GETTING YOUR CHILD
TO SLEEP

A Parei

GW00506587

GETTING YOUR CHILD TO SLEEP
A Parents' Guide

Dr Danny Wolf

Translated by Jennifer Crawford

BELLEW PUBLISHING
London

First published in Great Britain in 1991 by
Bellew Publishing Company Ltd
7 Southampton Place, London WC1A 2DR

Copyright © Danny Wolf 1991

ISBN 0 947792 57 0

Phototypeset by Input Typesetting Ltd, London

Printed and bound in Great Britain by
Billings & Sons Ltd

*This book is dedicated
to my beloved parents.*

Contents

Preface

If you look into the windows of bookshops, you will see among the different volumes displayed a great number which deal with paediatrics, theories of education, child psychology and the findings of many experts. But very few deal with the problems of getting children to sleep or with the constant crying which is often a prelude to going to sleep. Parents who are looking for an answer to their children's sleep problems remain uncertain even after reading such books. The treatment of sleep problems is time-consuming and, for this reason, many doctors are unable to deal with it comprehensively.

This book, by a paediatrician, will help you find answers to all your questions about children's sleep problems, from birth to puberty.

It is not meant to be a substitute for medical treatment, but it will certainly take the place of those questionable 'tips' which neighbours and friends give us; it will also take the place of so-called 'advisers' in many magazines and newspapers, whose advice usually lacks a scientific basis.

This book fulfils an urgent need for a comprehensive and systematic explanation of sleep, basing itself on proven medical and psychological foundations. Its approach is practical, and the effective methods of treatment and education discussed here have been tested by experts in many different parts of the world.

There are many people who start from the premise that sleeping difficulties in children will sort themselves out in time. This may be true, but in the meantime parents and other family members have to suffer. Sometimes learning about sleep and about the difficulties associated with it can help parents to cope, for in such a complicated and sensitive process as sleep, only experience, knowledge and understanding can overcome the innumerable problems and frustrations that lead to conflict, strife and disappointment.

Fundamentally I take the view that sleep and nourishment should be left to the baby's choice, though the parents also have their rights!

Parents have a right to lead their lives as best they can and, above all, they have the right to sleep at night. Happy, healthy parents mean happy, healthy babies, but parents can only be happy when life with their babies fits into their domestic routine, and their routine is not subordinated to the caprice of their offspring. The methods of treatment described in this book take account of the needs of the parents just as much as those of the baby. Babies' physical or mental health will not be disadvantaged because parents do not always bend to their will.

This book cannot, of course, guarantee an absolutely certain solution that is applicable to *all* children, but the scientific, practical methods given here are likely to contribute to the development of healthy sleeping habits in children – and therefore also their parents.

Do you know

- how much sleep children need?
- when children should go to sleep?
- when they should exchange cot for bed?
- when they are able to do without sleep during the day?
- up to what age they should use a dummy?
- up to what age they should be fed at night?
- when children's crying is a sign of real distress and when it can be ignored?
- when certain symptoms need medical treatment and when they can be dealt with at home?
- when you should call the doctor?

Do you know whether

- babies should be allowed to sleep in the parental bed?
- children should have regular periods of sleep from which there should be no deviation?

- children should be allowed to take all their toys to bed?
- children should be allowed to play in bed before going to sleep?
- children should be allowed to go to sleep with their bottle or dummy in their mouths?
- you should stay in the bedroom until a child has fallen asleep?
- children should be allowed to go to sleep with the light on?
- you should let two children sleep in the same room or if it is better to separate them?

Do you know what you should do when children

- suffer nightmares?
- talk in their sleep?
- walk in their sleep?
- won't go to bed?
- wake up at night?
- won't be separated from their mothers?
- get frightened before going to sleep?
- want to be fed in the middle of the night?
- bang their heads against their beds?
- have attacks of breathlessness?
- wet their beds?

Do you know how to teach children

- to sleep right through the night without waking up?
- to fall asleep by themselves, at the right time and without the help of their parents?

And, finally, do you know how parents can bring up a baby and still manage to get a few hours' sleep themselves?

In this book you will find the answers to all these questions and to many others that may be worrying you. This book is meant for you – the parents. With its help, you will be able to differentiate between what is normal, which does not need any particular treatment, and those sleeping difficulties which must be treated. With the advice given here – advice which is clear, detailed and written with scientific accuracy – you will be able to cope with most sleeping problems.

The mere idea that someone who is not a doctor should carry out treatment that normally belongs within the doctor's competence fills many medical practitioners with horror. But I think the time has come to abandon conventional ideas and to recommend parents not to shy away from treating their children's sleep problems themselves. Naturally this must be carried out according to the methods described here: their efficacy has been proven.

The suggestions here are meant not just for mothers but for fathers too, whose contribution to the development of their children is of great importance. The responsibility for the care of baby and child should rest with both parents equally.

And finally I wish us all – *Goodnight!*

Introduction

Normal sleep is a development of normal sleep habits.
There seems to be a sort of conspiracy among doctors and other experts in their insistence that, however many hours children sleep during the 24-hour period, it is always enough. According to them, children do not suffer from lack of sleep, and there is no need to worry about ill-effects on their health. Those expressing such opinions are not concerned if parents have long since lost the joy they felt on having their babies, and are on the edge of mental collapse . . .

Must we put up with this only because there is no danger to the health of our babies or to their development? Is there really no way of alleviating this problem? Perhaps we could anticipate the problem and teach babies correct sleeping habits? But if we do this, we might harm our babies. Is it not better for us parents to dance to our babies' tune and give in to their every whim?

How can we bring up healthy, happy babies while we survive on minimal sleep? Must it be like this? Is it somewhere decreed that some parents' lives should be made a hell? Naturally, the answer to these questions is an emphatic No. Were that not the case, this book would be unnecessary.

The main problem with most books on childcare is that they do not give advice that takes into account any changes in a baby's habits. Most authors regard babies' wishes as unalterable and start from the premise that 'they know best what they need'. However, those of us who are concerned with modern methods of treatment and upbringing have long been of a different opinion. Today, many experts agree that parents should not have to submit to their babies' every whim, but instead, they must learn to fit into the domestic life of the family.

And not only this. We cannot simply deal with a sensitive and complex topic such as sleep by employing new methods of upbringing, however advanced they may be and however much they bear on the problem. We must also understand the processes involved in sleep and master all their peculiarities and the difficulties relating to them. This is why most of the conventional advice contained in childcare books has not proved to be really effective. First, we must know what it is that we shall be analysing, and we must also understand the psychological and mental needs of children.

Sleep in children is influenced by three main factors:

1 The phases of psycho-motor development – that is, the stages of our children's mental and physical growth. There are different forms of sleep at different times of the night and at different ages, and these will show themselves by varying sleep times and, perhaps, varying sleep problems. (The time that babies spend asleep and the characteristics of that sleep bear no relation to adult patterns.)
2 The character and temperament of children.
3 Environmental factors and their influence, the form of upbringing and the way in which children are taught to sleep.

If we wish to tackle any sleep problems that children may have, we cannot change their developmental phases or their characters. However, it is quite possible to change the environmental factors affecting children and the methods of their upbringing and to adapt them as far as is possible to the sleep habits of the child. In this way, we can tackle the problems from both ends.

For example, it is the character of children that determines the number of hours which they spend asleep during a 24-hour cycle. It is therefore unnecessary to alter the number of hours of sleep – in fact, this can harm children. It is possible, on the other hand, to bring children up in such a way that they spend most of the night asleep without waking up.

To do this, you must find out what is normal for each particular age – that is, how much sleep is needed by a child of such and such an age. Then you must be clear about the particular sleep habits that you should teach children from the time they are very small babies onwards, and how you are to do this. Thus you will know what to do *and* what not to do.

To help you in this task, I will first summarize what is considered normal sleep, and the problems which occur with children of different ages. In so doing, I will examine the particular difficulties that are linked to the characters of individual children, and attempt to solve them. Finally, I will tackle the problems which result from the wrong sleeping habits. I have excluded medical problems: these should be left to the doctors.

1
Normal sleep

What happens during sleep?

You may be surprised to hear that, even today, science is largely incapable of answering questions about how much sleep people need and about the exact function of sleep. Even less is known about what causes dreams, their physical manifestations and their contribution to our health and well-being.

We do know that sleep consists of two main patterns:

1 *Active sleep*
This is the sort of sleep where the eyes often move to and fro, which is how it got its technical name: REM (rapid eye movement) sleep. This is the phase in which we dream. Breathing is irregular; and there is an increase in oxygen consumption; the regulation of body heat is disturbed; males may experience erections and females similarly may undergo sexual excitement. All the muscles of the body except those of the face, remain immobile, and there is an interruption in the transmission of stimuli between brain and body.

2 *Deep sleep*
The muscles are relaxed and the body is completely at rest. (This sort of sleep is not necessarily silent because snoring often occurs during deep sleep, when the muscles of the upper respiratory tract are relaxed.)

Sleep cycles

Sleep consists of cycles, each lasting 90–100 minutes. This means that an eight-hour night comprises about five sleep cycles.

When we first drop off, we sleep lightly and dream (active sleep). Then we enter deep sleep, which is composed of four sub-stages through which we descend until we reach the final stage of deepest sleep. After we have spent some time in this fourth sub-stage we return to the third sub-stage, then to the second and to the first, finally entering 'active' dreaming. Then we wake suddenly for a few seconds, turn around, change our position, check the world around us in a flash, and then once more fall into a new sleep cycle.

The sleep patterns of babies are not completely the same as adults, but they do resemble them to a large extent: 90-minute cycles, with each consisting of deep sleep and active sleep. In both adults and babies, if there are any abnormal variations in the brief interruptions in sleep between cycles, it may be so difficult to go back to sleep that genuine sleep disturbance occurs. It is during this intermediary phase of waking that several bad sleeping habits can arise: for example, with babies the habit of falling asleep with a bottle or with the help of parents, in their arms or in their bed. During this transitional period, children may wake up, become aware of the lack of what they have become used to and then, in moments, become wide awake. There is now a problem.

However, we must distinguish between problems such as this and others that are not connected with sleeping habits and/or external conditions, but are tied up with the personality of the child – for example, nocturnal fears, bedwetting and sleepwalking. These occur during deep sleep and not during the dream stage.

Sleep: a learned habit

Although sleep is one of our natural bodily functions, we are not born with fully developed patterns, or habits, of sleep. We gradually acquire such habits as we grow older and they are subject to many influences. To a large extent, our sleep mirrors our whole personality and its maturity. It can reveal personality disorders, but so can a personality disorder cause a sleep disorder. The way we sleep, like the way we eat, is part of our character, and it is influenced by habit, heredity and environment. Contrary to popular belief, sleep does not mean a suspension of all bodily activity. For one thing, the brain does not stop working; it is just redeployed, so to speak, to allow the muscles and other parts of the body (including certain centres of the brain) to rest. Controlling this interruption of conscious activity calls for extra work on the part of other brain centres.

The origins of sleep are in habit and behaviour – not behaviour as we would normally understand it, but in a primary and fundamental sense. It is not something which depends on our surroundings, but is a way of satisfying bodily needs.

Babies up to one year

During the first month of life, newborn children are in a state of semi-sleep. This is very like (though not the same as) real sleep, during which we dream and rest. Babies wake up whenever they have to satisfy their bodily needs – for example, in order to eat. It is from this beginning that they learn how to sleep.

It is a simple fact that each one of us makes sure we get the necessary sleep according to our age and biological needs. Sleeping patterns, habits, rhythms, the times we go to sleep and the depth of that sleep, the ability to go to sleep in strange or noisy surroundings, or conversely the inability to do so, the awareness of dreaming and of the extent of the dream world, the ability to wake up easily and fall asleep easily – all these are learned (or acquired) character traits. They are no different from other inherited traits or those which result from environmental influence, upbringing and parental care.

Newborn babies are motivated only by the compulsion to satisfy their bodily needs, but this is not just a matter of eating. It also has to do with mothers conveying a sense of tranquillity, harmony and love. A mother who follows her own natural intuition rather than imposed conventions is likely to satisfy all her baby's needs and help him or her to form good sleeping habits.

At first, babies are still unaware of the difference between day and night. They wake up whenever they feel uncomfortable from a wet nappy or whenever they are hungry, want a cuddle or for reasons that it is impossible to discover. This is one of the most difficult periods for the mother. She has scarcely recovered from the exhausting business of giving birth when she has to take on the burden of feeding and caring for the baby, and all this in addition to making meals, housekeeping and caring for the other members of the family, often with little or no help from her partner or others. Women are often anxious and depressed at this time, which may be partly due to their changed hormonal state. With her baby waking every two hours or even every hour, making it impossible for her to snatch even a few hours' uninterrupted sleep, it is quite understandable that a mother can be brought to the brink of collapse. She certainly cannot be blamed for mistakes or oversights. It has to be understood just how difficult her position is and that her capacity for tolerance is not at its best at this time.

The following points should encourage mothers:

- The period during which the baby takes no notice of time, when it does not distinguish between day and night, is limited to six to ten weeks.
- If the baby wakes up every two to six hours to be fed during the first six months, this is entirely normal.
- Babies who wake up every hour do not need to be fed each time! If they wake at intervals of less than two hours, an attempt should be made to soothe them in some other way. Babies do not need to be fed at such short intervals, and they will often stop crying if you simply pick them up. Naturally they will sleep if they are fed, but you will not be able to cope with such frequent demands, and in the end, your baby will not benefit. In some babies, it is even likely to produce an automatic reflex, a subconscious idea that they must be fed each time they wake, and they will suffer if their parents do not resist the impulse in the first place.
- This is a trial shared by every mother, and like all the others before you, you will probably find the strength to cope with it.
- You may tend to blame yourself for lack of experience,

or think that you are not yet mature enough to be a mother. You may be afraid that the baby is waking up every two hours because of some mistake you are making. You may worry that you won't have enough milk. Set your mind at rest. First, the number of times the baby wakes does not depend on you. It would not change even if you did things differently. Second, so-called 'mistakes' in caring for your baby at this period cannot cause him or her any future harm. Third, you should not feel at all guilty if you seem to have reached the end of your tether and, in pure despair, leave the baby to cry for a while. Just try to get over this time as best you can and as well as your strength allows; the baby meantime will make sure of getting what he or she needs. However, you should try not to blame other people for what is happening.

- You can rest assured that your baby is just as healthy and happy as one who sleeps the whole night through. This period provides no indication of the baby's ultimate character or human qualities. At this stage, it is impossible to influence character or personality. It is a time which passes without any help from others and has no influence on the baby's future.

- If you are tired and irritable, it is better to let your partner take a turn at looking after the baby during the night. He is almost certainly as capable of soothing him or her as you are.

- Sit down for a few minutes and think about the fact that your baby cannot possibly know how inconsiderate and intolerable his or her behaviour is. He/she cannot look at the clock, and has not yet read this book! Babies are not to blame for the fact that their mothers cannot adjust to their sleeping habits and are forced to sleep only when they happen to be asleep themselves. After all, the total time they spend asleep each day would be more than enough to satisfy their mothers' sleeping requirements. It is therefore sensible for you to use these breaks during the day to relax and sleep instead of following your inclination to do something else, such as housework.

Waking in the night and night-time feeding

Parents long for the moment when their babies will stop demanding a night-time feed. Giving up the night feed will be hailed as a significant stage in a baby's development, perhaps even more important than the appearance of the first tooth, growing out of nappies, the first attempt at walking or the first indistinct word. The night feed is often a reason for envying the neighbours. Sometimes it gives rise to arguments between parents about how best to break the child of the habit, and doctors are frequently consulted.

The advice which follows is designed to help you abandon prejudices, bad practices and old methods of childcare.

A baby's waking for a night feed does not depend on any particular stage of development and gives no indication of progress or lack of it. All babies have their own rhythms which largely depend on their character and needs. Just as with other human qualities, there are enormous differences in these between one baby and another, and a different rhythm should never be imposed. Contrary to popular belief, waking in the night is not at all influenced by the amount of food a baby takes at the evening feed.

During the period when a baby cannot sleep for more than six hours without being wakened by hunger or a wet nappy, it is better to get up once in the night than to have to get up too early in the morning. A sensible mother makes all the necessary preparations for the night feed in advance. It should be small and given as quickly as possible; afterwards she can resume her sleep undisturbed. Once the baby has grown out of the night feed and the parents are not wakened until early morning, many of them actually long again for the time when they used to get up briefly and then go back to sleep, sometimes without even remembering having got up!

It is useless to try to 'train' babies of this age by leaving them to howl for several nights so that they get used to not waking in the night. This approach is not only futile, but does babies considerable harm. So when does a baby give up the night feed, and how can you help him or her – and yourself?

Only babies can decide when they are ready to give up their night feed. No attempt should be made to influence them until they are six months old. It is best to accept things as they are and realize that they are really not so bad, either for your baby or for you. Of course, it is possible to try to wean babies from their night feed before the end of the first six months, but it is better not to. Anyone who would still like to try should turn to the section on the amount of food a baby needs at night (*see* p. 126).

If, however, a baby persists in wanting a night feed beyond the age of six months, or he or she expects several meals in the course of the night, weaning should be considered at once. In cases such as this, we are not dealing with a physiological need, but with a *habit* that should be broken as soon as possible.

Should children be allowed into their parents' bed?

This poses no problem at all until the baby is six months old. Before then, the question should be decided only as a matter of comfort. In general, babies do not want to sleep in their parents' bed, preferring their own cot. On going to sleep or waking in the night from a bad dream, babies may well look for the security of being near their parents, but they will still prefer to be in their own cot, their own familiar place of safety. They will be satisfied simply to know that their parents are nearby.

However, if children wake frequently, especially during the first months, parents often prefer, for simple convenience, to take their babies into their room and even into their bed.

But what about the situation from the point of view of the parents and their interests? While it does not disturb babies in the least to sleep in their parents' room during the first six months, this arrangement can be very disturbing for the parents, particularly if the mother or father is sensitive to noise. Whatever the case, the decision depends only on what the parents want.

In the second six months of babies' lives, they can be disturbed by noise round about them; their status as lodgers in their parents' room is therefore undesirable.

The second and third years

Babies gradually become less dependent on their mothers. They begin to control things in their environment. They develop their own personalities and willpower and can express these in words and movements. They also know that they have to please their mothers and do what they are told to do so that they can get what they want.

To toddlers of this age, going to sleep means separation from all the familiar things around them, from their daily environment and, above all, from their parents and the warmth, security and love they heap on them – all this in exchange for a dark and anxious sleep and especially for a sleep with which they are not yet really familiar! They cannot yet recall exactly what happened the night before, so it is hardly surprising that, in their heart of hearts, children dread being parted from their world, frightened that they might not come back to it the following day.

Can you blame children if they try as hard as they can to play for time? Eventually, of course, they will get tired and fall asleep. But to make this difficult task easier, and ensure that they have no problems sleeping during the night, it is important that parents make their children feel secure in an atmosphere of peace and calm, something parents can give them through their warm and natural love.

The development of children can be divided into several different phases, from the beginning of the last quarter of their first year up to the age of three. Each of these is characterized by fears and problems, but the solutions to these problems are specifically suited to the phases during which they occur.

By the end of the first year, babies are firmly attached to their mothers and are afraid of losing them. They are also afraid of strangers. It is important therefore that they maintain a relationship with the one particular person who appears regularly – usually their mothers – and that this person should surround the child with love, warmth, attention and the greatest possible sense of security, ensuring constant and unchanging contact with him or her. The fear of losing this key figure is an essential phase in the normal social development of every baby: the first 'anxiety period' *(see below)*. It dominates babies' feelings and determines their behaviour. Naturally, it is also mirrored in their sleeping problems.

To begin with, babies are afraid of losing their mothers (or fathers, or some other 'significant other'), but at this age, the concept of 'losing' means no more than being unable to see this person nearby. Later, babies become afraid of really losing their parents and, with them, everything associated with the home and all the things with which they are familiar. During their second year, small children will come to realize that their parents are simply in the next room and are not going to disappear altogether. When children reach the age of two-and-a-half, the bond with their mothers becomes even closer and deeper and they are entirely devoted to them.

The first anxiety period

During this period, which can last from 8 to 14 months, babies are so attached to their mothers that they are afraid of losing them. They cannot understand anything beyond the four walls of their immediate environment, and only believe in the existence and reality of what they can see. At this age, babies can learn to cope with this problem by themselves – but how?

Of course, it is hard for babies to change their ideas of what they see, but they do begin to realize that what they cannot see, what is no longer in their field of vision, *will* come back. This confidence is reflected in the way they behave and play, and it influences their sleep, too. The favourite game at this age is 'peep-bo'. Children will play it with all sorts of variations – hiding their faces, then peeking out again a moment later, enjoying seeing someone they know cover their face, then uncover it again. Children delight in this game and are happy to repeat its familiar gestures *ad nauseam*. As they do, they are reinforcing their faith that someone who disappears from their field of vision *will come back*.

Babies' thoughts find expression at bedtime, too. Between the ages of 8 and 12 months, because they are afraid of being separated from their mothers they cry a little, but it does not last very long and, in general, it is a good sign.

It is therefore important to allow babies to cope with this first period of anxiety on their own.

During this phase, you are right to harden your heart and leave your child to cry until he stops at his own accord. Once you have left the room, you must keep reminding yourself that, at this age, children's crying is 'experimental', brought on by separation from their mothers. If your child behaves like other children of his age, and bursts into bitter tears when you put him to bed and turn your back, you must not make the mistake of giving in to him. People often make this mistake, but it is apt to result in serious habitual problems. If you are worried about this, you should turn at once to the section on experimental crying (*see* pp. 32–3, 73–4).

The problem of fear of separation begins again at the age of two. During this phase, children are more attached to their mothers than ever. They are not so much afraid of their mothers disappearing from their sight as of not being able to stay with them. In addition, children who have not yet reached the age of three still cannot distinguish between dreaming and reality: everything that appears in their dreams seems real. For example, a two-and-a-half-year-old child who can already talk will assure you with complete conviction that what frightened her a moment ago was a real live lion attacking her in bed.

During this period, getting children to go to sleep becomes really difficult, and they must be helped to come to terms with this problem. Particular difficulties, and ways and means of solving them, are fully explained in Chapter 4.

From cot to bed

When is the right time to make this change?

As with every process of development, it is impossible to pinpoint any particular moment as the right one, but in general, the move to a bed is made when the child is three. However, if this proves difficult, it is better to postpone it for another year or so.

If children begin to clamber over the bars of their cots,

trying to climb out, it is advisable to put them into a bed as soon as possible in case they hurt themselves. In any case, it may be that the cot has become too small for the child: small children often feel offended at still having to sleep in a cot. In such cases, it is time to make the move.

Every transition and every change brings its own particular problems. Small children need a stable and familiar environment in which to feel secure, and this is especially true when it comes to the type of bed they sleep in. Their cot has been a stronghold during the most difficult hours of the day. It is the place in which they have spent more than half of their lives until now. It is what they are used to, and the place where they have learned all they know. It must be remembered that for children their cot represents the whole world. So to make things easier for them – and for yourselves – it is advisable to approach the move from cot to bed in the following way.

- Never force children to make the change. If the desire to move to a bed does not originate with children themselves, you can afford to wait right up until they are four years old, the easiest age for changes in sleeping habits *(see below)*.
- It is best to make the move when there is a relative lull in sleeping difficulties, and not as a way of trying to solve some other problem. It should also be at a time when there are no other changes taking place, such as moving house.
- Small children should never be moved into a bed in order to give their cot to a younger brother or sister.
- It is a good idea for children to be taken along when the new bed and bedclothes are bought, so that they can take part in choosing them.
- New beds should be installed in children's rooms for a few weeks before they start to use them, so that they can get accustomed to the idea. When the time comes, they will ask to sleep in the bed of their own accord.
- To begin with, it is a good idea to put children in their new beds just for naps during the day – when they are

less anxious than they are at night – and only 'promote' the beds to night-time use after a week or so.
- It is a good idea to put toys and favourite dolls into a new bed, to give it an attractive and familiar look in the child's eyes.
- Leave cots in children's rooms for a few weeks after the move.
- The goodnight routine should be observed in exactly the same way as before. Parents must be especially patient and loving at bedtime, while at the same time intervening firmly if their children make any move to get out of bed. It is a good thing to give children the feeling that they are now grown up and can be proud of their promotion. But they must also be made to understand that the absence of safety bars does not mean that they are allowed to get out of bed during the night. There must be no compromise about that!

Four- to six-year-olds

Four is a wonderful age, when all sleeping problems usually resolve themselves. It is the ideal age at which children are ready to cope with new experiences and to drop old habits. Sometimes it is worth using simple expedients to capitalize on this auspicious time. If difficulties have been encountered moving children from cot to bed and the procedure has been postponed until now, there is no need for regrets: neither children nor their parents suffer any harm as a result. Use the opportunity of this wonderful age to make up for lost time.

Reaching this propitious age, when many of their sleeping difficulties disappear, can give children the incentive to shed difficulties and habits they had before. But as with every dramatic turning point, extreme caution is needed. Not only are children about to make the transition to new sleeping arrangements but the change also commits them to a change of status. From now on, they understand that they are expected 'to behave like grown-ups' and to put away their old habits. Bearing all this in mind, each phase should be approached gradually and patiently, and parents should always 'keep their finger on the pulse' to make quite sure that the responsibility placed on their children is not too much for them and that they are really mature enough to take this burden on.

However, all children are different, and in a few weeks, the situation may change from one extreme to the other. Or perhaps this trick does not produce the desired effect in your child . . . In any event, children soon leave the age of four behind, and new things can begin to cause sleeping difficulties.

From seven to puberty

The years from the age of seven to the beginning of adolescence is what Freud called the 'latency' period. Unlike earliest childhood, which was full of conflict, change, character development and coming to terms with all things emotional, the latency period is characterized by mental and emotional tranquillity. At this stage, children turn their main attention to events at school, sports, social life and so on. After the conflicts of the preceding period, this phase of development is usually more settled. They sleep peacefully, not unlike an adult, the only difference being that children sleep for longer.

Lack of emotional equilibrium returns with puberty, and its repercussions are once more experienced as sleeping problems similar to those which appeared at a much younger age. Falling asleep becomes difficult again, sleep is disturbed, and dreams are powerful and can create anxiety. Two things in particular trouble the young person at this age:

- The first is the sex drive – the libido (sexual drive, the longing for caresses) – as the sexual impulse reaches its peak, prompting the urge to masturbate, often associated with feelings of shame.
- The second factor is young people's desire to prove to themselves and the world around them that they are now grown up – for example, that they can stay up at night as long as adults and even longer. They may also be beset by brooding fears about future problems, such as the

choice of a profession, the assumption of new responsi-
bilities and leaving the hothouse atmosphere of their parents' home. All this is bound up with the need to make
independent decisions.

2

The sleep process at every age

The daily wake/sleep ritual is divided into four basic components, each of which alters according to age: putting to bed; sleep; waking up; being awake.

The following are general guidelines on what can usually be expected of children at different ages. Remember, however, that every child is different, and your child's behaviour may vary occasionally, often or not at all from what is outlined here.

In the first month

Babies become tired and go to sleep after every feed. They sleep most of the time and wake about every three hours for nourishment. They cannot yet differentiate between day and night.

After one month

They start to differentiate between day and night. They wake up four or five times a day, less at night.

At 16 weeks

In the night

They sleep mainly at night, falling asleep easily and quickly after the evening feed. They wake between 5.00 and 8.00 in the morning.

Daytime sleep

Babies usually sleep between two and four times during the day, often divided into a morning and afternoon sleep, with one towards evening. The morning sleep, after a short feed, can almost be regarded as a continuation of the night sleep.

At 28 weeks

Putting to bed

Babies go to sleep easily after their evening feed. No problems with getting to sleep or waking up.

Sleep

Continuous, without problems.

Daytime sleep

Prolonged. Most babies go to sleep two or three times, mornings or afternoons, at fixed intervals. Some prefer a long morning sleep and a short one in the afternoon; with others, it is the other way round. An additional short nap can also occur at different times.

At 40 weeks (10 months old)

Putting to bed

Babies go to sleep easily immediately after the evening feed.

'Experimental' crying

Babies between the ages of 6 and 12 months usually cry loudly before going to sleep. They begin immediately their mother has turned her back to leave the room, and their crying lasts several minutes. This occurrence should be properly evaluated: that is, if something is genuinely wrong, it must be seen to; more usually, however, the crying, should be ignored. (*See also* p. 26.)

The isolated few who experience difficulty and distress in falling asleep and are used to crying need between 15 and 60 minutes' persuasion before sleeping.

Sleep

Most children in this age group sleep without a break until between 5.00 and 7.00 in the morning: some, however, tend to wake up for an hour or two between 2.00 and 4.00 a.m.

Daytime sleep

In the morning, after the bath and the 10.00 feed. This is the longest span of sleep during the day. There is a shorter afternoon sleep at about 3.00 p.m., after a walk or after play.

At one year

Putting to bed

They go to sleep without difficulty between 6.00 and 8.00 in the evening.

Sleep

Straight through the night until about 8.00 a.m. Sometimes babies wake up and yell. They can also be wakened by very loud noises or other disturbances. In some cases, they are restless, particularly when they first go to sleep.

Getting up

Between 6.00 and 8.00 in the morning. Babies wake up crying and call for their mother. After their nappy has been changed, they will lie in bed quite contentedly for another hour until breakfast.

Daytime sleep

Children aged between 12 and 14 months get used to sleeping only once during the day. The transition stage is gradual and differs with every child; parents simply notice that their children come more and more to dispense with their morning nap. While this is happening, many children find that, while two bouts of sleep a day are too much, one is too little: this is why they prefer to sleep between 11.00 a.m. and 1.00 p.m. These children should take their midday meal before going to sleep and they should be put to bed early in the evening, at 6.00 or before. They usually wake up very early on the following day.

Apart from the individual differences which characterize each child, there is another factor that should be taken into account: children learn to walk at this age and use up a lot of energy in making repeated attempts, so they easily get tired. It can happen that children who have gone over to sleeping only once during the day will once more need several periods of sleep a day.

Such a daily routine – or, more precisely, lack of routine – can, unfortunately, last a long time, much to the parents' regret, but it is possible in such cases gradually to bring about an alteration in the length of sleep (*see* Chapter 4).

At 18 months

Putting to bed

This usually happens between 6.00 and 8.00 in the evening. Children play with their favourite doll or teddy bear and then fall asleep.

Sleep

Children wake up occasionally in the night, particularly after having been involved during the day in some activity they have found fascinating. They calm down, however, and fall asleep without any difficulty. Every little sound will wake them again. Possibly they dream.

Getting up

Between 6.00 and 8.00 in the morning. Children lie in bed quietly until they feel that it is time to get up, and then they call for their parents.

The daily nap

This is taken after the midday meal. Although children take their favourite toys to bed, they quickly doze off. They sleep for about one-and-a-half or two hours, then wake without difficulty and begin their normal activity.

Two-year-olds

Putting to bed

Children do not go to sleep until between 8.00 and 9.00 in the evening. They make a great many demands before going to sleep: they want to take numerous toys and picture books to bed with them, and they employ different delaying tactics. For example, they may want to go to the lavatory again and again, to have a drink and so on. Sometimes they cling to their mother and do not want to let her go.

Sleep

Children sleep lightly, and are wakened by every noise (sometimes even without) and ask to go to the lavatory.

Getting up

Between 6.30 and 7.30 a.m. Children pass the time before someone comes to them quite happily, playing by themselves. If they call for their parents, it is all right to give in to them, changing their nappies if necessary, give them a biscuit and put some toys in their bed. Generally this is enough to keep them happy so that they wait patiently and in a good mood for their breakfast.

Daytime sleep

Toddlers aged from 21 months are generally reluctant to go to sleep, but some will play in their beds until they doze off. Sometimes, when children are ready to fall asleep but refuse to admit it, their parents have to keep laying them down and tucking them in. The length of sleep needed is even longer than that required by one-and-a-half-year-olds: 2–2½ hours. Many children find it difficult to wake up and, when they do, are rather confused.

With two-year-olds, the midday sleep is lighter and more superficial. Many older toddlers do not sleep at all during the day.

Most children do not need their parents to interfere in their daily nap, which lasts approximately two hours. It is not wise to waken children; they should be left to sleep until they wake up by themselves. Children who do not sleep during the day will usually play quietly and contentedly for one or two hours at the same time as they previously took a nap.

Two-and-a-half-year-olds

Going to bed

It is desirable that children should go to bed before 8.00 p.m. (and certainly not later), even if they have slept during the day. Going to bed is usually accompanied by an extended goodnight routine. Some children still ask for their parents even after they have said goodnight; others tend to talk or sing to themselves until they fall asleep.

Sleep

There are some cases of night waking or sleepwalking (*see* pp. 91–4). Sometimes children cry out in their sleep or talk. They wake frequently and, from time to time, go to the lavatory. These are common occurrences at this age.

Getting up

Most children sleep uninterruptedly until 8.30 or 9.00 a.m. If they wake earlier, they play in bed until breakfast.

Getting up: children aged one-and-a-half to three years old

Many children may deviate in their behaviour from that described above. There are some who wake up and ask to use the potty; they then refuse to go back to bed and insist on playing in their parents' room or parents' bed. Others agree to play in their own room but only under certain conditions and demand all sorts of things from their parents. At least one of the parents must lose sleep and give in to these demands . . .

Daytime sleep

At this age, the daily nap is a difficult problem. Many toddlers do not want to go to bed at all; others agree only when they have grown tired from playing by or on the bed.

One solution is to leave them in the bedroom of another member of the family, or in the living room, whichever they prefer. After they have become tired enough from playing and no longer refuse a sleep, they can be allowed to doze in the bed or on a blanket or cloth spread out on the floor. If this is not possible, and the problem can only be solved by shutting the child in his or her room, even at the cost of a quarrel, then you must be careful to lock all the windows so that the child doesn't come to any harm.

Waking from sleep can also be accompanied by difficulties. If children cry and yell, it is best to leave them on their own and go near them only after the storm has abated. Children who tend to wake up irritable and angry should be woken indirectly. For example, you should go into the room and open the blinds noisily without taking any notice of the child.

Three-year-olds

Going to bed

The goodnight routine can be shortened. Most children of this age take a doll or teddy bear to bed, at about 7.00 p.m.

Sleep

Nocturnal anxieties and nightmares are frequent. It is possible for children to talk in their sleep, or cry out, or even – still sleeping – crawl into their parents' bed or wander around the house. Children at this age are often able to tell their parents what they have been dreaming about: their parents, daily occurrences, parks, animals. Some dreams can wake children from sleep.

Getting up

Between 6.00 and 8.00 a.m. Children can be confused and apprehensive. They may call for their parents and ask to be lifted out of bed.

Daily sleep

Generally toddlers play happily in their room and remain wide awake. Those who prefer to sleep do this with fewer difficulties than when they were two-and-a-half years old. Waking is also no longer a problem.

Four-year-olds

Going to bed

Children go to bed willingly at about 7.00 p.m. They like hearing bedtime stories and occupy themselves for about half an hour with their books or toys. They take dolls or soft toys into bed with them.

Sleep

Children wake at night only to go to the lavatory and do not need any special help from their parents. They wake with a shock, but dream less frequently, and can give more details of their dreams. Their stories begin to sound quite plausible, even if they are a mixture of fact and fantasy.

Getting up

Between 7.00 and 7.30 a.m. Children wake up, climb out of bed and play in their room until breakfast.

Daytime sleep

Children between the ages of four and five-and-a-half usually fall asleep late in the afternoon. If they remain awake between 4.00 and 6.00 in the afternoon, they usually enjoy playing quietly instead.

Five-year-olds

Going to bed

Bedtime isn't always the same. Most children go at 7.30 p.m., others prefer 7.00, still others don't go until 8.00. Putting them to bed is not prolonged and there is no goodnight routine, though some children like to read or draw. On the other hand, there are some who doze off in their parents' bed or in the living room and are only later carried to their own bed by their parents.

Sleep

Approximately half of all children suffer from nocturnal anxiety or nightmares, which reach a peak at this age (*see* pp. 96–9). Generally they cry out during the night and this wakes them up. They and their world are disturbed by the strength and the depth of these phenomena. Many children remember the content of their nightmares and dreams, and, if they wake, they mix up this with stories from their own imagination. However, only a very few children of this age dream about normal, everyday events.

A third of children wake up and go to the lavatory in the night, mostly without the help of parents.

Getting up

They usually wake at the normal hour, about 7.00 a.m. or perhaps a little earlier. Sleep generally lasts about 11½ hours. At this age, the children go to the lavatory alone; they also wash and dress themselves. Only very seldom do they need the help of parents, and they sit at the breakfast table without being asked to. However, the differences between children at this age can be very great indeed. Some like to get up later, and a few can only be roused with difficulty between 8.00 and 8.30 a.m.

Five-and-a-half-year-olds

Going to bed

At this age, most children go to bed at 7.00, some at 7.30 p.m. Generally they do this without making a fuss, and fall asleep immediately, many within half an hour.

Sleep

They sleep right through the night. They still may have nocturnal anxiety and nightmares, though these do not cause the same distress as they do with five-year-olds. They may dream of something coming into their bed, lying in wait for them or attacking them. They often wake up in a panic and seek the comfort and safety of their parents' bed, where they recount their dreams. They certainly feel less vulnerable than five-year-olds, but find it difficult to shake off the nightmare. On the other hand, they can have pleasant dreams about everyday things. There are also children who talk in their sleep, shout out 'Mummy' or the names of other family members.

When they wake at night, children of this age need somebody who can stay close to them and reassure them. One solution might be to let children sleep in their brother's or sister's room (with the latter's permission, of course).

Getting up

From five-and-a-half onwards, getting-up time remains the same, varying only according to a child's character and when school starts in the morning.

Some children wake between 7.00 and 7.30 a.m., get up immediately, occupy themselves and come to the breakfast table by themselves. Others, however, are not able to behave in such an independent manner and need the help of one of their parents, sometimes until they are ten years old. Don't worry – the way in which your child gets up in the morning is no clue to his or her character and no measure of his or her independence.

Six-year-olds

Going to bed

Bedtime is usually between 7.00 and 7.30 p.m. though there are children who wait until 8.00 p.m. Generally children climb into bed and fall asleep immediately, but many sing, talk or look at a book for half an hour. Some like to have a short chat with their parents before stretching out in bed. There are also some children who like to take toys to bed and discuss the events of the day with their parents or listen to a story.

Sleep

At this age, most children spend the night in deep, uninterrupted sleep, though under some circumstances children can, while still asleep, creep into their parents' bed.

If children do run to their parents' bed, they may have been upset by a dream and must be comforted, until they feel brave enough to go back to their own bed. There are some who feel the need to stay with their parents a long time, despite the fact that the fear of a six-year-old is less marked than that of a five-year-old, and can be dispelled more easily. We must realize that these feelings of anxiety caused by nasty dreams are genuine and take pains to help children overcome their fear in whatever way they prefer. It is comforting to know that this phase will be relatively short. Yet we must differentiate between fear that is genuine and that which is false, for children can seek their parents' bed, awake or asleep, *without* being driven there by a bad dream and only because they want to sleep with their parents. If you are suspicious, then be firm! Clever parents know how to tell the difference between genuine and pretend fear. But even after a bad dream and a period of comforting, children should not remain too long in their parents' bed.

At this age, children can have pleasant dreams as well as unpleasant ones. They can laugh in their sleep and imagine that they are playing in their room.

Six-year-olds usually don't need their parents to help them to the lavatory. They often don't even feel the need to tell their parents. They simply climb quietly out of bed and go back when they have finished. Pretend you haven't noticed anything; you only need to mention it next morning if you wish to compliment your child on being so grown up.

Seven-year-olds

Going to bed

Bedtime is usually between 7.00 and 8.00 p.m. according to the family's habits. Not a great deal of time is spent over this. Children get ready for bed on their own and quickly fall asleep. However, they may sometimes read a book or listen to the radio or just lie there quietly for half an hour before nodding off.

Sleep

Many children at this age like to go to bed, and will sleep deeply and noisily for about 11 hours. Only a few have anxiety dreams, and these gradually cease. Waking and going to the lavatory is also less frequent. In general, children of this age group dream less, but when they do, most of their dreams are about daily events and friends. Often they will assume the role of their dream-hero, zooming through the clouds in an aeroplane, driving a car, walking on air and so on. If they have bad dreams, these are about being chased, about robberies, wars and monsters. Dreams like these are influenced by cinema and television, but they also often reveal the children's own violence and aggressiveness, particularly directed against parents. Films and stories about children being abducted and or attacked also exert a negative influence.

Eight-year-olds

Going to bed

Bedtime is usually later, about 8.00 p.m. Children tend to put it off and stay awake a bit longer. They get ready for bed on their own, lie down in bed and call out to their parents, wishing them goodnight. At this age, the preparations for going to bed are long and drawn out, and more time is needed for going to sleep than with seven-year-olds.

Sleep

This is more or less deep and noisy; only a few children have anxiety dreams. Some still wake up to go to the lavatory.

Most dreams are benign. The cinema, television and books have a considerable influence on them, particularly when they contain mysterious or fantastic elements (as in science fiction). Although seven-year-olds cannot defend themselves against the dreams caused by books, television and films, eight-year-olds *do* usually know when they should close their book or turn off the television in order to avoid undesirable consequences such as a bad dream. They often say: 'I don't want to see this, otherwise I'll be scared all night,' or 'Don't tell me that just before I'm going to sleep!'

There are wide differences between children at this age,

both as to what they dream and how they react. Not all children have the same dreams or the same number of dreams. Reactions are also individual. Many children love talking about their dreams and recount them time and time again. Others remain reticent. In any case, children do not like being woken up from a dream – they want to 'see' it to the end.

Nine-year-olds

Going to bed

Most children know themselves when it is time to go to sleep, though they like to stay awake a little longer to chat and have to be reminded several times before they finally decide to go. The time is usually about 8.00 p.m.

Sleep

Sleep is usually quieter at this age than it is with eight-year-olds. Children play major roles in their own dreams, which are about daily worries, duties and playmates. Frightening dreams usually deal with natural phenomena such as storms, or they involve being chased or threatened or some action such as swimming, flying, being whirled around quickly. These dreams are still strongly influenced by cinema and television. Children know this and are reluctant to see films that will give them bad dreams.

Ten-year-olds

Going to bed

Usually between 7.00 and 8.30 p.m.; somewhat later on holidays and after special occasions. Most children in this age group must be reminded to go to bed, sometimes more than once. They try to gain time by making all sorts of excuses such as 'I must finish my homework first,' or 'I want to see the end of this TV programme.'

Before going to sleep, they may listen to the radio, read

or just think about the events of the day. Boys usually fall asleep more quickly, usually within half an hour, whereas girls tend to like to stay awake longer in bed, perhaps for up to an hour.

Sleep

Children of this age sleep straight through the night, without waking, although bad dreams are frequent. If you ask a ten-year-old boy whether or not he dreams, he will answer, 'Why do you ask? Everybody dreams!' At this age, bad dreams are more frequent than pleasant ones, and are usually about monsters and other strange creatures, robbers, etc. Children may dream about being kidnapped and taken prisoner, being hunted and murdered. They may also cry aloud in their sleep. Some children are reluctant to talk about their anxiety dreams.

Getting up

Most wake up without difficulty at about 7.00 a.m., wash themselves, get dressed and have breakfast. But there are some who like to sleep longer and should be encouraged to get out of bed.

Eleven-year-olds

Going to bed

Bedtime is usually about 9.00 p.m. (7.30 to 10.00 p.m.). With many children, it depends on what is on television, but most have fixed times for watching programmes. The repeated reminders from parents – the 'battle over bedtime' – are all part of a game, but this can lead to disagreements. Some children like listening to the radio before falling asleep, some brood and some read.

Sleep

Many children dream. Although there are more pleasant dreams than unpleasant, nightmares are violent and frequent. Bad dreams don't normally wake children out of their sleep.

Children in this age group usually tend to tell their dreams more readily than at other ages. Dreams are concerned with the daily routine: homework, pets, sports, cars, etc. The average length of sleep is about 9½ hours.

Getting up

Usually about 7.00 a.m. Most children like lazing around in bed for another quarter of an hour; about half prefer to sleep longer, and have to be reminded to get up from time to time, and occasionally scolded. Most children sleep much longer at weekends.

Twelve-year-olds

Going to sleep

Bedtime is the same as it is for eleven-year-olds – that is, about 9.00 p.m. Most go to bed willingly or ask permission to stay up a little longer, usually in their own room. They listen to the radio there, read or even do their homework. Most children say that they go to bed because their parents force them to, not from their own choice. Most lie awake in bed for half an hour or an hour, or listen to music and daydream before they go to sleep.

Sleep

They generally have fewer dreams, still fewer bad ones. They are also more reticent about them. Themes are: daily events, friends, things they have done. The dream is often a mixture of school, the family home or the house of a school friend, etc. The average length of sleep is 9½ hours.

Getting up

Usually about 7.00 a.m. Many children have an alarm clock and stay in bed for another half an hour. Others find waking very difficult and need their parents' help. But normally they are aware of the responsibility of getting up at an appropriate time and do not want to be late for school. At the weekend, they can sleep as long as they like.

Thirteen-year-olds

Going to bed

Bedtime can be any time between 8.30 and 10.30 p.m., usually about 9.30 p.m., but later following special occasions, on weekends and during holidays. Bedtime also depends on the habits of the family. Most children of this age group know when they have to go to bed and don't need to be coaxed. But when it's a question of a particularly interesting event, such as an exciting television programme, children will try to 'bargain' with their parents. The actual bedtime itself is not controversial, so normally there are no differences of opinion; therefore, if children ask to stay up later, parents should show some understanding. Many children stay in their own room in the evening and decide for themselves when they should put out the light. Like seven-year-olds, children of this age love their beds and their sleep. Many children need about half an hour to relax in bed and like listening to music.

Sleep

Rather more anxiety dreams than with the twelve-year-olds, but they are less significant than the pleasant ones. Many dreams revolve around the daily routine, and concern sport, trips, school and so on. The children call their dreams 'crazy', 'funny', 'weird'. As a rule, the number of dreams decreases. While they sleep, these children scarcely make a sound, and almost never wake up. There is, however, one particular group of children who breathe so loudly when they are asleep that you can hear it quite a way off. The average sleep lasts 9 hours.

Getting up

As with twelve-year-olds.

Fourteen-year-olds

Going to bed

Like those a year younger, the majority of fourteen-year-olds spend the evening in their rooms. Bedtime is usually between 9.30 and 10.00 p.m. Most need about 15 minutes to get ready for bed. The children decide for themselves when they go to sleep. Most do this because they are tired, others because that's when they always go to sleep. Only a few have to be reminded. Normally they behave like adults. Most of them, especially boys, fall asleep promptly; others need another half an hour in bed relaxing. The wish to listen to the radio is less marked at this age than previously. Most think about the day to come or make plans; others remember homework and the lessons relating to it, or think about other daily matters, or people they admire, or about love.

Sleep

In this age group, the difference between children becomes noticeable – that is, between those who sleep deeply and do not wake up at night, and others who are wakened by the slightest noise. There are also differences between those who get up early and those who get up late, and in the hours of sleep needed, although, on average, children of this age sleep for 9 hours. Half report having a few anxiety dreams. Normal dreams are not about daily happenings, but about the fantastic: magicians, magic tricks and supernatural events. The dreams are confused, strange and remote from reality.

Getting up

Getting up at this age is very problematic. Children seem to need more sleep and it is difficult for them to get up in the morning.

Fifteen-year-olds

Going to bed

Bedtime is between 10.00 and 10.30 p.m. Teenagers are quite independent about everything to do with sleep. Many organize their sleep pattern with their schoolwork in mind – that is, how much time they need for their homework – or they calculate the time they need for spare-time activities. Others are more conventional. Like children a year younger, these relax in bed for half an hour before falling asleep. There are no problems about going to bed, but getting them up the following morning can be a real headache.

Sleep

Fewer dreams, fewer descriptions of dreams, no anxieties or nightmares. Many of these teenagers show an interest in the effect of dreaming on their psyche and in the psychological interpretation of dreams. They sleep restlessly and often thrash about in bed, kick the air, throw their arms around, but they don't wake up, and the next day they don't talk about having had nightmares. The average length of sleep is 8½ hours for girls and 8¼ hours for boys.

Getting up

This is a problem. Most rely on the alarm clock, while those who sleep late are woken by their parents.

Sixteen-year-olds

Going to bed

At this age, there is complete independence, and individual variations are more important than age limits. Boys tend to go to bed earlier than girls, generally because they want to conserve their strength and stamina. Girls go to bed about 11.00 p.m. (between 10 p.m. and midnight), while boys usually go about 10.30 p.m. (between 9.00 p.m. and midnight), and both go later at weekends or on holidays. It takes boys longer to fall asleep than girls.

Sleep

The need to relax, daydreams, the degree and type of dreaming, difficulties in getting to sleep – all these factors are determined by teenagers' characters, not their age. According to the descriptions given, all their dreams are pleasant, especially when they concern school friends, colleagues, members of the opposite sex and excursions.

Children's sleeping habits: a summary

When you look at this table, you should remember that it consists only of average measurements; they are not meant to be regarded as binding, or as the only normal times for going to bed and sleeping. A 12-hour average means that one child sleeps for 14 hours whereas another – and this could be *yours* – only needs 10 hours.

The day and night cycle

Some experts have suggested that there is an interesting reversal between a child's behaviour during the day and what he or she will dream of at night. 'Good' takes the place of 'bad' and vice versa. In other words, if a child, in his parents' opinion, behaves well during the day, he or she will have bad dreams at night. Good behaviour in this case means that

Age	Bedtime	Hours of sleep
1–1½	6–8 p.m.	10–12
2	8–9 p.m.	9½–11½
2½	7–8 p.m.	11½–13
3	7 p.m.	11–13
4	7 p.m.	11½–12
5	7–8 p.m.	11–12
5½	7–7.30 p.m.	11½–12½
6	7–8 p.m.	11
7	7–8 p.m.	11
8	8 p.m.	10½
9	8 p.m.	10
10	7–8.30 p.m.	9½–11½
11	7.30–10 p.m.	9–11½
12	9 p.m.	9–9½
13	8.30–10.30 p.m.	8½–10½
14	9.30–10 p.m.	9–9½
15	10–10.30 p.m.	8–8½
16	9–12 a.m.	7–10

a child is at ease with him/herself and his/her parents, is not aggressive and does not need to be scolded.

The cycles, which persist until the age of 11, go something like this (according to age):

- *21–24 months*: good days/bad nights
- *30 months*: bad days (this is the time when children tend to be 'defiant')/good nights
- *3 years*: good days/bad nights
- *4 years*: bad days/good nights
- *4½–5 years*: good days/bad nights with anxieties.
- *6 years*: a lot of trouble during the day/generally good nights, not many nightmares, and not much anxiety even if there are nightmares
- *7 years*: good days, although there may be grounds for apprehension and worry/good nights, but periods of anxiety when falling asleep

- *8–9 years*: trouble during the course of the day/no problems at night, few fears
- *10 years*: good days/anxiety at night
- *11 years*: bad days/much better nights

How to tell if children are getting enough sleep

The answer to this question can be found in your children's waking rather than their sleeping state. If children are sufficiently active, if they are not sleepy, do not tend to follow you around and don't react to things nervously, crossly or impatiently, you can be assured that they are getting enough sleep, even if you don't think they are sleeping 'as long as it says in the book'. Sleep should not be measured by the clock but only by how tired children actually are.

The lack of sleep in children can manifest itself in many different sorts of behaviours – for instance, hyperactivity, irritability, difficulty in concentrating, forgetfulness, problems at school or general laziness.

3
Encouraging proper sleeping habits

Although some sleeping habits are preferable to others, there are very few hard-and-fast rules that apply to every situation. Nothing succeeds like success, so if the sleeping habits that you have fostered in your child prove to be effective, if you and your child are happy with them, and he or she goes to sleep easily and seldom wakes during the night, if he or she gets enough sleep and shows no sign of being tired or overly excited or irritable during the day from lack of sleep, your methods are the right ones and you can stop reading this book now. However, if your child has difficulty sleeping or wakes frequently in the night, you might just gain from reading further.

There are some sleeping habits and ways of promoting them that are better than others, and if you adopt them, you will have a much greater chance of making sleep easy for your child and safeguarding him or her against future sleep problems. For example, after you say goodnight to, say, your eight-month-old baby boy and go to your own room, you will be creating a problem that will prove very disruptive in the future if you allow him to think that you are going to come back, give him a bottle, pick him up and play with him until he goes to sleep. This kind of stimulation will make going to sleep much more difficult for him.

If your child is a little older, you may find even worse sleep problems. If, for example, you continually take your baby girl into bed with you, even if it is nice for parents as well as baby, the habit may eventually give rise to a lot of psychological problems. One day you will inevitably have to break your child of the habit, and it will be far more difficult.

If your child is 'absolutely terrified' of going to sleep, you may think that you are 'solving' the problem by taking her into bed with you. However, you will eventually realize that all you have done is merely swept one problem under the carpet and created another. There must be a reason for your child being so afraid, and you can best help her by exploring the reasons for her exaggerated fear and helping her find a way to overcome them. This is bound to be a difficult and lengthy business and may well call for considerable patience and firmness on your part. You may even have to take professional advice. But even all that is better than taking the child into bed with you and momentarily enjoying the best of both worlds . . .

Occasionally parents choose to take children into bed in order to solve their own problems! This may occur, for example, in a one-parent family, or if one parent works nightshifts, doesn't come home from work until late at night or is often away on business. If the parent at home is suffering from tension, he or she may find it comforting to have the child near him or her in bed. After a row or when one partner is not in the mood for sex, he or she may take the child into bed as a defensive measure. *Under no circumstances should a child be used as an instrument for solving his or her parents' problems.* Anyone who feels it is helpful to have a child in his or her bed should first think carefully about what really lies behind the feeling, and deal with it without burdening the child.

Another thing: while it's true that I am in favour of children sleeping when they need to, and of parents accommodating their children's wishes about when they should sleep and not forcing a strict timetable on them, this can only go so far. There are limits, and there are good reasons for them.

As you will see as you read on in this book, I believe that children need to be brought up consistently, even if this calls for some strictness on the part of their parents. Moreover, Nature has given human beings immutable, natural, biological clocks which encompass a 25–26-hour day. We are all familiar with the experience of, on days when we do not have to work, going to bed an hour or two later than usual, and getting up later the next morning. If we were to rely just on our instinct about when we should go to bed, instead of looking at the clock, the result would be to lengthen the 24-hour day to 25 or 26 hours. We would go to bed every evening an hour or two later and the next morning get up relatively later still. Children of one and two have no concept of time, so we must be careful to put them to bed at the same time each day, otherwise we could find that their sleeping time becomes longer and longer, at the rate of an hour a day. The results would not be hard to imagine . . . Children expect their parents to prescribe the order of their days and, in this matter, strictness is preferable to inconsistency.

To foster good sleeping habits in your child, it is worth observing the following guidelines.

Consistency

Children who are put to bed at the same time every day will accept this as natural and will not offer any resistance to it. On the other hand, children who are put to bed at different times will find it very hard to get used to going to sleep at a particular time. While it's true that very young children cannot tell time, they do have internal biological clocks and will feel much better if the activities of their day are arranged in accordance with this. Parents must therefore help their children to synchronize their biological clocks to our precision quartz watches. Routine and order act as important safety valves as children develop; they ensure that children get good, healthy sleep which gives them temporary respite from the shocks and events of everyday life.

Many parents rebel against a philosophy that has anything to do with consistency, firm boundaries, a daily routine and so on. They want to be modern, to embrace freedom; they don't want to be narrow-minded, restricting their children within all sorts of conventional boundaries from the day they are born. But I would like to point out that it is much easier to bring up children who are subject to regulated sleeping times and a daily routine – even if this routine is broken from time to time on birthdays and other special occasions. When they become adolescents and adults, such children are much more flexible and ready to adapt to any given situation. And what is more important, they experience no difficulty or anxiety in getting off to sleep.

If children cry and refuse to go to sleep, there is nothing more harmful than inconsistency in their parents' reaction. For example, one day parents might let their child stay in the living room until she goes to sleep; the next day, they might play with her in her cot until she lets herself be parted from them; the third day, they might leave her to cry because they have decided she must be taught not to; and on yet another day, when they are in an impatient mood, they may show her their annoyance by snapping at her. No baby can understand this sort of behaviour or learn not to cry because of it – which is, after all, what we want. Behaviour such as this can only confuse him or her. If we suddenly show our children that we can be strict, they will see this as some kind of punishment for a misdeed they are not aware of having done. Moreover, babies always expect us to treat them in a placatory way, and behave accordingly. So every time we suddenly demand good behaviour of them, we add to a cumulative experience of *destroyed expectation*. The result is that our babies never know what we actually expect of them nor the right way to behave.

Bedtime and duration of sleep

It is difficult, in fact almost impossible, to make children sleep for longer than they actually need. You cannot make a child go to sleep if he is not tired, and it is just as undesirable to keep him awake if he is tired. Every child needs a different amount of sleep, and we must try to ensure that our children get the sleep they really need. An arbitrary sleep quota – whether based on something you have read in a childcare book, on a friend or neighbour's experience or even on your own experience with your other children – must not be imposed.

Parents may be worried by the fact that their children remain happily in bed, busy with their toys and prattling away to them until late into the night. They will try to make their children go to sleep, in blatant contradiction of their physical needs. Such attempts induce behaviour which can develop into a real problem, just as with the difficulties over feeding. Besides, if parents try to persuade children to go to sleep when they are not tired, the children may come to believe their parents simply want to get rid of them. They won't be able to understand why their mothers and fathers don't want to have their company when this means so much to them! Children who have been forced to go to bed can develop complexes that will make them hate their beds. The same is true of eating, but it's worth remembering that sleep is inherently less attractive than food, since it is much more boring and a cause of greater anxiety.

It is in the nature of sleep problems that they tend to grow worse and worse until a vicious circle is established. Lack of sleep makes both children and parents tired, nervous, impatient and liable to irritation and loss of temper at the slightest provocation. All this only exacerbates efforts to induce sleep.

When children are not tired but their parents demand that they go to sleep, it is usually the children who emerge victorious from the ensuing struggle, particularly if there has been a head-on confrontation. Besides their conscious pleasure at their 'victory', subconsciously these children may feel insecure because of fears and doubts about their parents' ability to bring them up. They become disillusioned by their inability to deal with general problems as well as specific ones related to behaviour. The parents, too, will suffer guilt and anxiety because of their failure to solve their children's sleep problem.

Contrary to general opinion, it is not true that, by putting children to bed later at night, this will stop them from waking so early in the morning! What is true is that if children have a long sleep in the afternoon, they will not be tired in the evening and will not feel like going to sleep until late at night. But if their daytime sleep is reduced, they will not function well in the afternoon, and there will not usually be any difference in the way they sleep at night.

As children get older, bedtime becomes later and later. This is what children naturally expect and parents are generally sympathetic. The bedtime is later because children need less

sleep and are less tired. Parents are also influenced by friends
and acquaintances setting later bedtimes for their children
and may follow their example. It is difficult and pointless to
fight against established norms.

Feeding and sleeping

There is hardly a single food that is not credited with properties that influence sleep in one way or another. There are
foods that are supposed to have soothing and soporific
effects, and others that, it is claimed, keep people awake.
There are even some supposed to do both!

Milk, for example, is credited with soothing and sleep-
inducing qualities. On the other hand, milk is also supposed
to cause wind and intestinal discomfort in babies and have
a disturbing effect on their sleep. Television advertising
promises milk drinkers relaxation, and this is certainly the
popular view, but reliable research has been unable to confirm that a mug of warm milk is better for you in the evening
than a mug of warm water.

Grape sugar is also supposed to have either 'mentally and
physically stimulating' or 'calming and soporific' effects. All
that has been proven is that neither milk nor grape sugar
improves the state of your teeth, if you take them before
sleep.

Drinks containing caffeine – such as coffee, cola, etc. – do
cause sleep problems and frequent waking in the night, but
apart from these drinks, it has not yet been proved that any
food influences sleep. Use your own discretion: if some foods
'work' well for your child, just carry on with them. Don't
expect to solve sleep problems by having your child adopt a
new diet every so often. Apart from the nutritional harm
that a sudden change of diet can cause a baby, any change
in what he or she eats is likely to have a bad influence on his
or her sleep, since what is needed is consistent and balanced
nourishment.

Dummies and thumbsucking

Thumbsucking has been a normal activity in babies since time immemorial; to parents, the dummy may be the invention of the century! No one has yet fathomed the real reason why babies suck, but in all probability, it is a physiological and psychological need which one should not struggle against. On no account should young children be stopped from thumbsucking. The activity gives them an immense amount of comfort, and surprisingly, there is no damage to the teeth until the adult ones come in at the age of six or seven. Babies may swallow some air while feeding if nothing comes out of the teat that they are sucking, but contrary to what many people think, a baby can suck a dummy for hours without swallowing any air at all! It's also quite unnecessary to boil a dummy every time it falls on the ground; just rinse it in ordinary tap water. After all, you don't boil your child's thumb every time he or she touches the floor with it! And, of course, dummies should never contain or be dipped in anything sweet.

The family and a child's sleep

Many parents are so concerned about the well-being of their children that they will not allow their children to be alone. They go into their room far too often to reassure themselves that they are 'all right', that they are breathing normally, that they haven't pushed the bedcovers off and so on. These frequent visits of inspection only serve to disturb children and wake them up. Sometimes children will even stay awake on purpose, waiting for their parents to return to their bedside.

In households with two parents, both should take turns at putting children to bed. If they don't, problems can arise if, for example, one parent is ill or busy, or the mother is in hospital giving birth to a new little brother or sister. Children who have become accustomed to being put to bed exclusively by their mother will not be prepared to allow someone else, even a loving father, to take over this role.

Cooperation between parents, in this and all other things,

is absolutely vital. Children quickly learn to exploit their parents' reactions, to capture their full attention and be spoiled and coddled. For example, if one parent comes home late and wants to play with the child after the other has put the child to bed, the latter will learn that this is the time to make up to the just-arrived parent and reject the other's presence. This sort of behaviour not only makes for problems in getting children to sleep, but can also lead to subconscious envy and quarrels between parents. So while, of course, late-arriving parents can play with their children, it should not be after they have been put to bed, nor in a way that may accentuate any conflict of interest between mother and father.

If there are two or more children in the home, it is not a good idea to put them all to bed at the same time. Older children should be put to bed later, in recognition of their greater maturity. In addition, older children should also be allowed time alone with their parents, so that they feel that their parents are devoting themselves wholly to them. (The parents must, of course, do exactly the same with younger children.)

Babysitters

Be careful about babysitters when your children are between 8 and 14 months old. At this age, babies develop a fear of strangers and are afraid of losing their mothers. I can recall numerous cases where children have woken up in the night and found themselves confronted by a babysitter whom they have never set eyes on before; since the mother was not there either, the babies suffered a severe shock on waking.

In cases like this, children run the risk of developing traumatic sleep disturbances. It is important therefore – especially at this particular age – to make sure that babysitters are known to children and that they are present for about an hour before the children go to sleep and take part in putting them to bed.

Rocking a child to sleep

Up to the age of about three months, this is the best method of sending babies to sleep, and should be used whenever they do not go to sleep of their own accord. From three months on, however, babies know how to lull themselves to sleep, often by means of a repetitive, monotonous movement of the body. So leave them to do the job themselves; stop rocking them, so that they do not come to expect it.

Sleep and the fear of death

Sadly, I have known quite a lot of children of four and older who have been haunted by fears and nightmares because they have not had death explained to them in the right way. At this age, children are strongly affected by ideas about death, and we must, therefore, be careful about the attitude we convey to them about it. How should we explain death to children? Or, more specifically, what should we *not* tell them?

First and foremost, we should never compare death with sleep. Many parents choose precisely this analogy to convey the idea of death to their children. They say, 'This person has gone to sleep for ever,' or if they are asked what a dead person looks like, they answer: 'He looks as if he is fast asleep.' Obviously these types of responses can only lead children to identify sleep with death or at least to the idea that you die while you are asleep. After imagining this sort of thing, it is not surprising that some children become afraid of going to sleep – they don't want death to take them by surprise in the night.

A comfortable and welcoming environment for sleep

If we are tired enough, most of us can go to sleep anywhere, in any position. But in a normal state of tiredness, it is harder to go to sleep if circumstances are less than comfortable. The prerequisities for sleep are relative quiet, a pleasant room temperature, darkness and so on, as well as a feeling that bed is a *good* place to be.

Sometimes an unexpected problem crops up during the transition from one season to another. When summer begins and the extra blankets or duvet that has kept a child warm all winter becomes too warm and causes sweating, you must change over to summer bedclothes. Even though the child may not object, and may even welcome the change, suddenly he can't go to sleep. Once you have realized where the problem lies, it can be easily overcome. This is an example of how, if you always keep an eye out for sudden changes, even if they seem insignificant, you can successfully deal with sleep problems.

Excessive warmth and sweating cause not only discomfort and occasional problems with getting children to sleep, but they can also result in tiredness. Not long ago I was treating a six-year-old boy whose parents complained that he woke up tired and lethargic in the morning even though he slept a good nine hours, and he would yawn and complain of being tired and sleepy all day long. After inquiring into every detail of this child's sleeping habits, I found the key to the puzzle: he slept all night long under an electric blanket that was turned up to the highest temperature setting. When he got up in the morning, the whole bed would be soaked with sweat and the bedclothes had to be taken off daily to be dried and aired. That was why the child was tired! Sweating uses up energy and is tiring work if it goes on for nine hours. The boy did sleep well, but he had to 'work' all night and was exhausted when he got up. When the electric blanket was removed, the child certainly had difficulty in getting to sleep at first, but then he slept well and got up every morning fresh and relaxed for the first time in months.

Excitement and anticipation of a birthday or some other treat makes sleep difficult for both adults and children. Remember sleep reflects our inner composure, and in babies, it is also to a great extent a reflection of the parents' composure. In the same way, exciting activity before bed makes sleeping difficult.

There is no better way of dealing with sleep problems than devoting the hours before bedtime to peace and quiet, relaxation and rest. By this, I mean the hour or two before the evening meal. During this time, all children, but particularly those who are experiencing sleep problems, should be prevented from becoming involved in games which excite them; frightening films and suspense-packed television programmes should also be avoided, and even exciting stories, and excessive physical exercise, are undesirable. A different problem can arise if one of the parents comes home from work late in the evening. Understandably a child's only encounter with his father or mother is apt to excite him or her just before bedtime, so ensure that the meeting takes place in a calm, relaxed atmosphere. A warm bath before bed is a good idea, too; it will calm children and make them sleepy at the same time.

Bed should never be used as a punishment or a means of imprisonment! And, for the same reasons, you should never use expressions such as 'That's enough! You're going straight to bed!' or 'I've had enough of your nonsense – get to bed *right now*!' or 'You've hit your sister, so you're going to bed!' or 'No television tonight, you're going straight to bed!' Children are quite capable of interpreting phrases such as these to mean that *bed is a place where you are deprived of freedom.* They may develop problems about everything to do with going to bed, when they should see bed as somewhere pleasant and peaceful, a home and refuge where they feel safe and comfortable.

Emphasizing the positive

Even in extreme cases of sleeplessness, always emphasize the positive in children's behaviour and play down the negative as far as possible. Children are not to blame for not being able to go to sleep nor is it an act of defiance or a way of putting pressure on parents. Since it is a matter of real inability, the parents' most important task is to help their children through the crisis, not to punish them for it. However, sleeping difficulties are never cleared up by an energetic, head-on approach. The root of the trouble is usually to be found in the symptoms of sleeplessness, so you must aim at an indirect, positive solution.

If, for example, a child has spent an almost sleepless night crying, when she wakes up after a brief morning sleep, you should say, 'What a nice smile you have this morning! I do like it when you say "Good morning!" so nicely.' Saying something like this will encourage children, strengthen their self-awareness, their optimism, their belief and hope that they can manage to sleep in a way which suits both them and their parents. Only by reacting in this way can you get the best results with children. They will then try to please you and will keep on making efforts to satisfy you and win your approval.

If, on the other hand, you can't overlook trivial matters and cope with your disappointment at having a night's sleep ruined, children will become discouraged, too. Their self-awareness will be undermined still further, together with their confidence in being able to do what their parents want. Children must always be praised, even for trivial things which are really quite obvious. Don't be miserly with praise and compliments – children need them! Be nice to them, so that they will behave better and be happy.

Bedtime and child development

It is important to realize that the time before children go to sleep provides a unique opportunity for parents to help form their personalities – for good or ill. This is the right moment to talk to them about all sorts of things and to discuss any difficulties they may have had during the day. Just before going to sleep, children are usually open to contact, ready to listen to what you say to them and to take suggestions to heart. You should therefore talk to them in a warm, sympathetic way, show them that you understand them, listen to their problems and try to reassure them carefully and gently. Under these circumstances, children will practise activities important for their development: they will try out their fluency and powers of expression; they will learn songs and stories by heart. The going-to-bed ritual will be transformed into part of their everyday lives specially set aside for practising such things. In the resulting atmosphere of peace and relaxation, contact with other family members is at its closest, and the exchange of experiences and feelings is at its most intimate. With a little attention and understanding, it is quite easy to achieve a great deal, and it is an effort for which parents will be richly rewarded in the end.

Sleeplessness and medical drugs

Sleeping pills should be used in children only as a last resort. Some parents consider drugs necessary and some doctors prescribe them fairly freely, but they should be considered only in cases of emergency – for example, to treat sleep disturbances caused by illness or which have already assumed unbearable proportions.

The following should be noted if it is decided to administer sleeping drugs to a child:

- Sleeping pills should only be prescribed by a child's doctor, never given by well-meaning friends or neighbours.
- If it is agreed that a child needs to take a drug to help with sleep, the dose must be sufficient to bring about the desired effect. Since doctors are often not convinced of the need to prescribe such drugs and do so only under pressure from parents, they may content themselves with a low dosage which has only limited effect. This makes matters much worse: children are given medicine they do not need; the medicine does not have the desired effect; and meanwhile, drug dependency and other undesirable side-effects may be engendered.
- Another tendency which causes great harm is the readiness of parents and doctors to use low-dosage drugs for a very short time. Since doctors, as I have said, may not be convinced of the need to prescribe at all and do so only under pressure from parents, they may try to limit the effect of the drug by recommending that it be used only in emergencies. In practice, however, the result is that the parents, who are not keen on giving tranquillizers to their ' children either, use the medicine only for 'fire-fighting' – that is, only in cases of dire necessity – and afterwards they are conscience-stricken and inclined to stop using the

medicine. It is important to realize that, once you have
agreed that your children should take tranquillizers, and
provided you have a medical prescription for them, you
must administer the drug to your children in the correct
doses and continue to do so consistently for at least two
weeks or longer. Only if you do this will the children be
able to develop a normal rhythm of undisturbed sleep at
night.

- As with adults, the effect of sleeping drugs on children is
  not uniform. There are people in whom tranquillizers
  produce the opposite reaction from that expected: instead
  of being calmed, they become wide awake and anxious.
  The use of such drugs must therefore be adjusted to suit
  the reactions of the particular child. Obviously, you have
  to get a doctor's advice first.
- The decision as to whether or not children should be given
  tranquillizers always involves an element of subjectivity.
  Clearly, doctors will be influenced in making their judgement by the amount of pressure exerted on them by parents. On the other hand, parents should refrain from
  'heroic' behaviour, such as not giving their children a
  medicine for which there is a real need. Tranquillizers
  taken over a period of two weeks or so can help children
  overcome long-term sleeping problems and tensions.

The side-effects of other drugs

I want to say a little about the side-effects of certain other
medicines not defined as sleeping drugs.

Almost everyone is aware of the soporific effects of antihis-
tamine tablets. These drugs, which were initially developed
for the treatment of allergies and skin irritations, have been
exploited for a long time for their soothing properties and
have been transformed from anti-allergy drugs into tranquillizers. However, we know less about the side-effects of other
drugs, particularly those which act as stimulants. Many
people are aware of the fact that a cough medicine such as
Actifed contains active ingredients which are both soothing
and soporific; on the other hand, it is not so well known
that these medicines also contain active ingredients which

can stimulate a child and cause sleeplessness, excitability and nervous irritation. As a rule, it should be remembered that even the 'simplest' of medicines, often those used to treat coughs, contain active ingredients which can be unbeneficial and even harmful.

If such symptoms as excitability, sleep disorders, nervous irritation and so on appear while you are giving your child cough medicine, you should seek your doctor's advice. Do not forget that cough medicines, unlike antibiotics, do not cure the illness; they only alleviate the symptoms. If the harm caused by side-effects outweighs any advantages, you should stop using them.

Another group of medicines which can have a significant effect on sleep are those used for alleviating asthma. Most have a strong stimulant effect, and using them can result in side-effects such as excitability, inability to get to sleep, nightmares, frequent waking in the night, trembling of the limbs and anxiety. Unlike cough medicines, they cannot be stopped without the doctor's permission, but it may be that a smaller dose or a change of medicine will diminish the side-effects. In some circumstances, a doctor may recommend that you just try to put up with them until the child's condition improves.

4

Common problems in children with normal sleeping habits

Sleeping problems can be divided into two categories:

- 'normal' problems – those that will cease spontaneously as children grow older;
- pathological problems – those that will disappear only with treatment.

Most of the sleeping problems mentioned in the preceding chapters were 'normal', and this chapter will review and enlarge on this category. Pathological problems are considered in the next chapter.

'Normal' sleeping problems are those connected with the psycho-social and physical development of the child. They are not caused by any outside factor, but appear of their own accord at any time, and take a similar form in many children. Since they are connected with the child's stage of development and have not been caused by an external influence, *they will also go away of their own accord without any treatment*, provided, of course, that parents react properly and do not allow the problems to become habitual, or introduce other circumstances which will make them habitual.

The boundary between 'normal' and pathological is not always clear, and both types of problem can even appear in the same child. For example, when a child who has been afflicted by a pathological sleeping problem reaches the age when 'normal' development-related problems begin, the two types can merge and exacerbate one another.

'Normal' problems are not necessarily easier to deal with than pathological ones. On the contrary, it can sometimes be much harder for children to get over a normal problem because the knowledge that it is shared by many other children and will go away even if it is not treated consoles parents to some extent and actually makes it more difficult for them to come to grips with what is wrong.

Most sleeping problems are caused by parents; they don't exist naturally. In 'primitive' tribes, children have no problem; they simply go to sleep when they get tired. Understandably, in our modern society where the everyday necessities of life are much more complicated and demanding, we cannot give up completely the conventional divisions of time. As usual, the solution lies between the two extremes.

The sleeping difficulties and problems of children are exactly the same as those their parents suffer. Children cannot be suspected of creating them on purpose to annoy their parents or to get their attention. The truth is quite different: the children suffer far more as a result of their problems than their parents. The latter should therefore be particularly considerate towards their children and help them to overcome their sleep difficulties. Don't worry – just about everything passes in time!

Below you will find a list of 'normal' development-related sleeping problems as they appear at each respective age.

In the first month

The disrupted sleep that characterizes the first weeks after birth can be unbearable for babies' parents, even if the problems are 'normal'. I have tried to comfort parents by giving them an objective picture of the difficulties which dog their efforts and suggesting ways of overcoming them. For example, what should parents do if their babies wake up more often then once every two hours?

I do indeed recommend that babies should be fed if they indicate that they are hungry, but scientific research has shown that babies do not need food more than once every two hours. So if they are used to feeding every hour, the length of time between feeds should be increased. For instance, the breast or bottle should be given every 75 minutes (instead of every hour), and then the intervals increased by half an hour each day until they have reached 2½ to 3 hours. This will not do babies any harm; they do not need to be fed more often. You will notice that the crying this causes soon stops, and that, in the course of the first three months, babies acquire a regular sleeping rhythm. Babies should be fed at night as long as they want, even up to the age of six months, but if it is important that the night feeds end after three months, parents should follow the step-by-step guidelines on pp. 128–9.

It is quite normal for babies to confuse day and night during the first period of their lives, but after the first few weeks, a determined effort should be made to change this, by fostering the right sleeping habits. This can be started from as early as one month. Of course, babies may continue to confuse day and night up to the age of six weeks, but if they have reached one month without showing any intention of going over to a day-and-night rhythm, then it will do no harm to begin their education even at this early stage, so that they will have learned to make the distinction by the age of six or seven weeks.

Parents should begin by waking their babies every couple of hours during the day and playing with them to increase the time they are awake before and after each meal. At night, however, the intervals when they are awake should be kept as short as possible, and making them especially pleasant should be avoided. If babies wake up in the night, a light should be put on in the corridor instead of the one in the bedroom. They should be breast or bottle fed and then immediately put back to bed so that they will go to sleep. Take care to change nappies quickly and only if they are really wet.

By keeping night-time contact short, parents may have to put up with a few minutes of heartrending wailing that wakes the whole family and even the neighbours, but they must not give in. They must not pick their babies up or sing them to sleep or try to comfort them in any other way. This is the only method that will ensure that parents and their babies will have peaceful nights in future.

Another thing that parents should start to do now is to give their babies their evening meals at the same time every day. Do not be afraid to wake them up for it, and if they sometimes wake up too early, leave them in bed, even if they cry. If parents stick to this routine, their babies will learn to get used to it.

If parents find it hard to wake their babies in the afternoon, this can be done step by step. Begin by waking them up a little early from their afternoon nap and then wake them a quarter of an hour earlier each day. Do this even if the extra time is 'wasted' in crying. Babies will gradually learn to transfer their longer sleeping period to the night hours, and in a short time, they will develop the normal 24-hour rhythm.

Babies over the age of six weeks

If your baby has got used to the day-and-night rhythm of sleep, and if you have weathered this most difficult time satisfactorily, then there are much better times in store for you. You may have painted yourselves too rosy a picture of these better times and may not be as satisfied as you had imagined you would be with the relative peace you now enjoy but, objectively, it can be said that now the baby has no real problem going to sleep or sleeping.

If problems do arise, they are the parents' problems – having to wake up during the night because their children cry for a long time or do not sleep enough. They may find it hard to attend to their children's needs at night and then be in a fit state to work the next day. But I know from my own experience that the problems encountered now generally have to do with parents' fears and uncertainties about their babies' health, and perhaps also a little to do with their impatience and lack of tolerance of their 'crazy behaviour'.

In some case, these uncertainties can also be – with justification – the result of parents' nagging doubts about whether the methods they are using to bring up their babies are the right ones. When children cry for hours, refuse to go to sleep and wake up repeatedly in the night, many worried families ask themselves whether they could be guilty of mistakes or of failing to satisfy all their children's needs – after all, it is easy to draw comparisons with the child next door who sleeps quietly and whom one never hears howling.

Unfortunately, I cannot give you any advice about how to get up in the night and still be fresh and bright for work the next morning. However, I can solve many problems and lay doubts to rest with a few simple words: at this age, babies do not suffer from 'insomnia'; they do not have educational problems and they don't want for anything. Perhaps parents do make mistakes with their children's upbringing or feeding or in setting their sleeping times, but not only do these so-called mistakes have no effect, for the time being, at this early stage, they do not even manifest themselves. It follows that the answer to 'sleeping problems' does not lie in caring for babies or toddlers differently, certainly not in giving them more food. Babies who wake up in the afternoon because of 'cramps' or 'wind' or who wake repeatedly in the night crying as if they were being roasted on a spit are healthy! They don't need anything and they aren't always suffering either. At any rate, experience has shown that no medicine will help solve the problem. Parents should not worry, either, that their babies have psychological problems, nor should they be so afraid of spoiling them that they go from one extreme to the other and adopt strict disciplinarian methods, leaving their children to cry all night 'so that they get used to it and learn their lesson'.

Please note this fundamental rule: there is no substitute for the tenderness of a loving parent who radiates calm. Pressing your baby tenderly to your breast and rocking him or her to sleep will be very soothing for him or her. You don't need any help from a bottle!

For babies of two or three months, a source of light for them to look at, or a brightly lit room in which they can play, are likely to soothe them and send them to sleep. By about the age of one-and-a-half, children are able to send themselves to sleep. The methods they develop usually involve being able to rock themselves to and fro or suck their fingers or play with a doll or even with a familiar piece of cloth, and they will use the same method if they wake in the night.

Many children of about one-and-a-half do not need their

parents' help at all to go straight back to sleep after they have woken up in the night. Some need a little assistance, but for the majority of these a little attention is enough: being picked up, rocked to and fro or given a bottle of (unsweetened!) water – all these will send them straight to sleep again. At this age, there are no troublesome sleeping problems. If children have wind and cry for quite a long time, or wake up crying in the night, this is not a sign of illness or distress; it is simply natural behaviour. You should therefore think of these apparent 'sleeping problems' as habits rather than problems.

'Experimental crying': 6–12 months

Imagine the following scenario: a baby is quite happy to be put to bed, but as soon as her mother turns her back on her to leave the room, the baby breaks into heartrending, sometimes tearless weeping. We know from experience that this crying is not usually a sign of real distress and that normally it stops quite quickly. Many people believe that this sort of crying is 'experimental': babies start to cry to see how their parents will react. If the 'experiment' is successful and the parents come back into the room and pick up the babies, the latter will repeat these outbursts regularly.

Other experts believe this crying to be a sort of relaxation technique practised by babies to make themselves tired and able to go to sleep more easily. However, whatever the reason for it may be, it is advisable to leave children alone to cry in their beds. Within a few minutes, the crying will stop and you will not have capitulated to the 'experiment'.

Only a few babies persist with this 'experimental crying' and turn it into something genuinely habitual. They will cry for up to half an hour, but if their parents do not give in, the crying will diminish after a few days to only a quarter of an hour, and finally to only ten minutes. Very few babies are able to cry indefatigably for hours over a period of weeks, making a considerable volume of noise, and sometimes crying so much that they make themselves sick. Only in such severe cases should parents try to interrupt their babies' crying, and when they do, they must be careful to prolong the going-to-bed routine and stay with their babies as long as it takes for them to fall asleep quietly.

Fear of separation from parents

This condition is similar to 'experimental crying' and is treated in a similar way. There are even experts who do not distinguish between the two phenomena. It occurs some time around the end of the first year, when babies are afraid of their mothers leaving them no matter for how short a time, and react by protesting. They are also afraid of strangers. They refuse to go to sleep, regardless of whether it is day or night. They don't allow their mothers to leave to go shopping or even to leave them alone to go into another room. This sort of behaviour goes back to babies' primitive fear of their mothers 'disappearing' – that is, going away without them and not coming back. If babies can't see their mothers, then for them the mothers have indeed 'disappeared' out of their world, a world restricted to the four walls of their room.

At this age, when babies' intelligence is not yet developed, they need their mothers to be physically near them as proof and reassurance that they really do exist (and are still nearby even when their children can't see them). The larger concept – the belief in the reality of unseen things – will only develop a few months later. Until then there is a real problem for babies – and, of course, for their parents, too. Naturally babies can't wait for months until their intelligence is sufficiently developed for them to understand what is going on beyond the four walls they can see. They explore the problem of disappearance and reappearance in the most active way and undertake endless experiments with it. We might find the industry of these little investigators admirable if *we* were not their guinea pigs. We would also be much happier if they would restrict their experiments to the daytime. But – although it would contribute greatly to the progress of a baby – we find it very hard to stage demonstrations of our presence and absence at two o'clock in the morning – a time when we can hardly tell what we are doing ourselves.

It would be appropriate to anticipate things a little here and point out that we are not really dealing with a genuine problem at all. Unlike the difficulty parents will be faced with later when their children reach the age of two, the separation difficulties that babies experience now are only related to their mothers and fathers and not (as with two-year-olds) to the whole world they inhabit. When parents encounter the later phenomenon, they will have a clearer idea of what 'experimental crying' really means. In more practical terms, they will realize then that parents and their babies share a series of problems which must be faced together.

How should parents react to these separation problems, to make it easier for their babies to overcome them? Should parents stay near their babies all the time in order to gain their confidence?

Even if this were a realistic possibility, in my view parents would achieve the opposite of what they were aiming for. Their babies would be deprived of the possibility of coming to terms with their fear of separation, and would not learn to use their own resources to overcome the first fear of their lives.

So how should parents act?

Experienced parents say that it is not wise to rush to comfort a baby at the first murmur of protest – even at this early age. Babies know how to cope by themselves with any particular situation they find uncomfortable. If they burst into tears when they are put to bed, the best thing for parents to do is to turn their backs resolutely and leave the room. If they do this, the sobbing will be shortlived and the babies will be able to overcome it without outside help. If, however, parents let their feelings get the better of them, and they try to comfort their young ones in some other way besides talking to them *in the babies' bed*, they are losing track of their objective – for two reasons: if parents behave undecidedly, babies may get the false impression that they really do have something to worry about and that their parents share this worry; and babies will not be able to get used to the fact that their beds are the safest places in the world. But if babies are left *in their beds* and are comforted there, they will soon come to recognize that this really is the best place.

It is, however, a different matter if the crying persists for a long time and the babies are in real distress, have genuine fears, are suffering pain and so on. Then, of course, they must be soothed and comforted.

At the end of the first year and the beginning of the second, anxiety at being separated from their parents (usually their mothers) makes babies uneasy, and we must respect their right to protest about it! But this unease and the attendant protest are a vital part of their development. We must make it possible for them to cope with it *themselves* – provided that this takes place *within acceptable limits!*

If parents rush to help their babies every time they protest about some trifling matter, the children will never learn to cope with discomfort or be able to develop a minimal ability to tolerate pain. Which brings us to an important question: how much should a baby be allowed to suffer so that he or she can develop a reasonable degree of tolerance?

You can know this only after you have put your baby's tolerance threshold to the test, as follows.

A reasonable amount of crying is good medicine

Babies should be helped and comforted only if their crying degenerates into fear and genuine distress – parents can judge this for themselves without being given any guidelines. At this age, the mistakes that parents make have more to do with giving too much assistance rather than too little. It is generally better to leave babies to cry until they get tired. Crying like this usually lasts only a few nights, and even within this relatively short timespan, it will be much less from one night to the next. *The main thing is not to waver!*

One more word of warning: because of the fears that babies have at this particular developmental stage – fear of strangers and of being parted from their parents, even if only for a short time – this is the most unsuitable age for hospitalizing babies or exposing them to different surroundings occasioned by outings or other changes of scene, although the latter may seem less worrying to parents. If fate decrees that a baby must go to hospital at precisely this age, every effort should be made by the parents to stay with him or her until the child comes home. Of course, parents can take it in turn to keep vigil or call in other close relatives to relieve them. Today most hospitals allow one parent to stay with the child in the ward, so parents should not have any difficulty in this respect. When the hospital stay is over, the difficulties it will have caused the child must be borne in mind, and so parents should make allowances for any difficult behaviour. But in doing so, they must at all costs avoid promoting the development of new unpleasant habits.

What should you do if your one- or two-year-old wakes up during the night? The job of calming babies who wake in the night, crying and shouting with fear, naturally falls to the parents. At this age, waking up does not cause any real problem, but it can easily become one! One of the parents should show the baby that he or she is there: simple physical presence and eye contact will satisfy the child. *He or she must get that, but no more than that!*

Whatever the situation, it is far better to avoid taking babies out of their beds rocking them or taking them 'for a walk'. Neither should they be diverted with toys or food or the like, for if one-year-olds are indulged with such treats, they will have every reason to want to stay up or rebel against going to sleep. However, the very worst way of indulging babies who have woken up is to take them into their parents' bed. This generally happens because the parents prefer, simply for convenience, to cut short the time that their babies stay awake – after all, they are tired, too – and so they take their children into bed with them as a guaranteed solution. Babies who had really needed only a comforting glance from one of their parents or a few soft words of encouragement while being gently stroked back to sleep – and all this, mark you, while the babies remained *in their own beds* – now entangle themselves and their parents in additional problems:

- The stimulus of being next to their parents is sufficient to wake babies and prevent them going to sleep again.
- The enormous pleasure that babies experience in such close contact with their parents encourages them to stay awake for longer and longer each time they are put to

bed. The by-product of refusing to sleep has proved so tempting for the babies that they can now not react in any other way. Their reactions are purely subconscious and not calculated to make their parents cross or to exploit the situation.

Putting babies to bed in a brother or sister's room

It does not matter what the age difference is – even a three- or four-year-old child who is afraid of going to sleep alone may be soothed by the presence of a brother or sister who is a few years older. The presence of these older siblings is often much more effective against babies' night-time fears than that of their parents. Some parents may perhaps be unwilling to take this advice seriously because they find it completely illogical. But believe me, it is much more logical than it seems and, what is far more important, it can sometimes work wonders and solve problems when much more ingenious methods have failed.

Big brothers or sisters will, like their parents, usually be wakened by the baby's crying, but unlike many parents, they won't pick the baby up but will content themselves with saying a few encouraging words or perhaps even a few short ones, before going straight back to sleep quite untroubled. Usually this peremptory sort of comfort is enough for babies and allows them to forget their fears quicker than might be believed, allowing them to resume a calm and unbroken sleep. A few months later, a return to the previous arrangement (the children sleeping separately) can be tried, but only after parents have carefully 'tested the water'.

It may be that older brothers or sisters do not take kindly at first to having little brothers/sisters put to bed in their room. But something can be done to overcome that, too. The elder children must be given the impression that they really are *big* brothers/sisters and must take care of younger ones. They can be rewarded for their help by being allowed to stay up for half an hour longer than usual. In many cases, older siblings will cooperate without difficulty – in the end, it depends on their parents' diplomacy skills.

I know from experience that parents need not be afraid

that their older children might not yet be mature enough for this role. It often happens that they are jealous of their little brothers or sisters and enjoy pestering them a bit during the day, but in spite or perhaps even because of this, the younger children develop enough respect for their older siblings to let themselves be comforted by them during the night.

Coping with past mistakes

What should parents do if they have not read this book in time and have already made the mistakes described and now have to face the consequences?

- Should they continue to give in to their children?
- Should they suddenly become strict and stop giving in?
- Or should they gradually stop giving in?

Such cases can be extremely difficult to deal with because there is a real problem which has taken root over a long period of time. Of course, the parents' behaviour cannot be abruptly changed, even if it is wrong. There is no single miracle cure to be recommended and it is best to seek the advice of a specialist in each individual case.

To show what can happen, let me describe one of the cases I have treated. It concerned the only child, an 18-month-old girl, of two educated, professional people. The mother told me: 'My daughter has never been a good sleeper. She has never slept through a single night since she was born. Recently we have been spending four hours every night trying to get her to sleep and we are already on the brink of physical collapse. What should we do? We have tried everything . . .' In answer to my questions, she went on to say that when she and her husband began to look after their baby, they 'could not bear' to hear her crying. They would go to her bedside several times each evening before she went to sleep. They would take her out of bed in the middle of the night, feed her and play with her until she went to sleep again. If she stayed awake longer, they would take her into bed with them in the middle of the night so that they could get some sleep themselves. Lately, even this no longer helped . . .

This was an ordinary healthy baby, whose repeated

waking, even though she was one-and-a-half years old, was perfectly normal. The problem lay in the length of time she stayed awake and her excessive demands while she was awake. There was no doubt that the problem was her parents' fault: they offered her far too much stimulation and pleasure every time she woke at night. Instead of comforting her by talking to her in her own bed, they took her out of bed. *The baby's problem developed out of the fertile soil of 'experimental crying' which her parents found so unbearable.* After deciding to leave the room, instead of allowing the baby to cry herself to sleep, they kept coming back again and again and comforting her because they could not bear her tears. In professional terminology, the baby's problem can be summed up as: a normal problem had become a pathological one.

The baby had developed a habit which had to be complied with before she could to to sleep. This habit comprised the whole ritual described above and provided a motive for her to wake up at night and an excuse for transforming every brief, spontaneous wakening into a ritual.

A child like this can be treated in one of three ways:

1 by training in gradual stages
2 by training in one single stage
3 by resorting to tranquillizers for a short time to alter the child's habits when going to sleep.

Generally speaking, alternatives 1 and 2 are preferable and they are described in the next chapter. In this case, however, I chose alternative 3, because it was a particularly difficult problem and also because I felt that the parents would not have been able to carry out the other methods. I prescribed a large dose of a tranquillizer which the baby was given every time she woke (and which took effect in 20–30 minutes). She continued to wake up during the night, but gradually became less active, while the length of time she stayed awake became shorter and shorter. Within two weeks she was satisfied with soothing words and being stroked in bed. After a further week, a kiss from her mother and a light caress contented her. At this stage, the medicine was stopped and the baby slowly returned to a normal routine. After about a month, she no longer woke in the night.

Sleeping positions

There are still two situations to be mentioned which can sometimes give cause for concern. They may sound like curiosities but they are not.

At a certain age, babies learn to roll over in bed from their stomachs on to their backs, but they are not yet able to roll on to their stomachs again. This often happens during the night, and babies then cannot go to sleep because they are used to sleeping on their stomachs and cannot get back to that position. Parents should not be cross with their children, even if they repeat this rolling-over operation several times during the night and each time parents have to get up and put them back on to their stomachs. Rolling over is a new lesson which the babies are 'studying', and parents have to adopt an understanding attitude towards these experiments; babies are quite entitled to practise everything they have learned. As yet the babies simply do not comprehend the relationship between rolling over and their problem with going to sleep, but this comprehension will come, in time.

A similar problem may develop when babies are a little older and learn to pull themselves up into a standing position in their cots. However, even though they can manage this, they will not yet be able to return to sitting or lying down. This problem is similar to the first and should be treated in the same way. These babies are practising something they have just learned, and it is quite right that they should do so. Unfortunately this usually involves calling on parents' assistance. The worst situation is when babies prefer to do their practising at night. However, parents should not show their annoyance but help their children with their favourite preoccupation even if they persist with it several times a night. Simply put them back into a sleeping position and then say goodnight.

Whatever happens, *children must go to sleep without help*, otherwise a new ritual will be introduced without which they won't be able to sleep. Sometimes parents, hoping to put a stop to these seemingly endless experiments try to help their babies to go to sleep in some way, such as putting them gently into a sleeping position and holding them there for a while. This is a disastrous initiative because it is important not to devote too much time and attention to children when they should be sleeping.

Crying in older children

I doubt the existence of parents who are not made uncomfortable by their children's crying. If the crying is very loud and persistent and also sounds 'convincing', it makes virtually all parents feel nervous and troubles their consciences. But Nature invented crying to arouse strong feelings in others, so who can blame parents if their children's crying makes them unhappy and they cannot ignore it?

The major question is, of course, how long can a child be left to cry. Unfortunately, there is no standard, unambiguous answer. Still, I would like to offer some advice.

Parents must learn to distinguish between one sort of crying and another. Crying that is the result of illness or discomfort, anxiety or fear must be dealt with appropriately, but that is not what we are concerned with here. Children over the age of one are capable of expressing their problems in their own way. They know how to indicate that something hurts or itches, by pressing the uncomfortable spot or scratching themselves. It is a pity that so many parents, who know that their children's crying is not caused by illness, often turn to their doctors and ask them to examine the children instead of taking advice on how to handle their fits of crying. It is even more regrettable that doctors who know that the crying has nothing to do with a physical illness, satisfy themselves with a brief physical examination and then turn their attention to their next patient.

Crying caused by anxiety occurs for different reasons at each age: fear of being parted from parents, fear of the dark or even fear of dying. Sometimes the child's reason is something as simple as being afraid of not finding his or her toys again next morning. These are all real fears which can be expressed in prolonged crying, and rather than trying to treat the crying itself, parents should try to give their children the help they need to overcome their fears.

Everyday fears and anxieties can be expressed both by outbursts of crying before bed and children's refusal to go to sleep. The only solution in such cases is to let the children roar at the top of their lungs, even if it is heartrending and so deafening that the neighbours comment on it. Don't worry – the problem will solve itself within a week or two, and often in just a few days, provided, of course, that it is not caused by a great fear or serious distress, or pain or illness. The refusal to go to sleep can persist even when children are very tired. In such cases, parents must ensure that they behave with consistent determination and even rather strictly. They must remember that, in this sort of crying, children are expressing all the feelings that have been suppressed throughout the day. The determination and firmness of their parents will help them overcome this problem within a reasonable time.

What happens if this sort of crying is not handled correctly?

Some parents are particularly sensitive to their children's tears and wails. They feel anxious and uncertain and are alarmed every time their children cry and reproach themselves when they make the slightest sound. With parents like this, every occurrence of normal crying, instead of being a small problem, becomes a family tragedy, influencing their everyday lives, and it always becomes worse. Exaggerated fear of their children's crying very quickly leads to *inconsistency* (and, by the way, sometimes to quarrels between parents, too). They take pity on their crying babies and hurry to their side. If their sympathy doesn't help, they try being firm, but they always relent too soon, and so the cycle repeats itself *ad infinitum*.

Sometimes parents think they can stop their children's crying by waiting until late in the evening before putting them to bed. I have to warn such parents that their children may be so tired by then that they are no longer able to go to sleep.

A paradoxical state can also result in a child's subconscious, below the level of awareness. Let me illustrate:

children expect decisiveness, a firm hand and energetic leadership from their parents to allow them to stop crying *of their own accord*. If parents then behave contrary to children's expectations – that is, hesitantly and inconsistently – they make it harder for the children to recognize parental authority. The result is a lack of trust and subconscious insecurity, which may show itself in a number of ways – in eating difficulties, for example, in bedwetting and so on.

Crying which parents think is caused by anxieties should be treated as follows. After an extended goodnight ceremony, which could include soothing words as well as chat, storytelling, gentle music and so on, the parents should leave the room, but not before they have made their children understand clearly that they will see their parents again after they have been to sleep. If the children then burst into tears of fright, they should be reassured, but *from outside the room*! It is important to give children a feeling of security and the conviction that they are not being abandoned and that their parents are very close by. But parents should not enter the room again. The sense of security given to the children, and their parents' consistency and firmness will bear fruit in a very short time.

An exception to this routine is when there is excessive crying that lasts more than 20–30 minutes. This can make children very tired and nervous, which in turn stops them going to sleep. It is sensible therefore to go and soothe such a child for a while and then leave the room again.

Sometimes there are particularly obstinate and difficult cases (which are also quite rare) when, despite all this, children are still afraid of going to sleep. In this instance, parents should act as follows. After the goodnight ceremony, when the children have been to bed and have been given the sense of calm that they need, the light should be put out (although a small nightlight can be left on if necessary). One parent then stays for a while sitting in a corner of the room. He or she should occupy him/herself with something, perhaps reading by the light of a torch, but he/she must not talk to the child or pay him/her any sort of attention, even if he/she cries or wants him/her. At the start, the parent should stay sitting by the child for about 30 minutes after he/she has gone to sleep. The reason is that the child often wakes after only a few minutes and looks for the parent. The quite genuine fears of separation which disturb some children's nightly rest can be dispelled in this way. Over a week or two the child will cry less and less and he/she will get used to sleeping normally.

Rhythmical movements and other monotonous activity

Rhythmical movements are perfectly normal phenomena, appearing when children are between one and two years old. Although these movements generally do not last long, they can persist in some children up to the age of four. If they go on for a long time or continue after the age of four, a doctor should be consulted. All rhythmical and other monotonous movements – turning the head or shaking it to and fro, rocking the whole body back and forth, or letting the head knock against some hard surface – are basically the same phenomenon taking different forms in different children (rather like the various forms of fingersucking).

These movements invariably come into play before children go to sleep and they become part of the going-to-sleep process, exactly like other routines associated with sleep. It is very rare for such movements to occur during the day (although it does happen). Sometimes children prop themselves up on their hands and knees (as if to crawl) and sway their bodies to and fro for hours on end. This swaying can rock a bed so violently that it 'walks' right across the room, and in blocks of flats downstairs neighbours often come up to complain. Babies can also be quite vigorous in bumping their heads or knocking them sideways against the sides of their cots, resulting in bruising.

Doctors don't agree on why children carry out these movements, but whatever the reason – be it play or the desire to combat boredom or tiredness or even some deep psychosexual phenomenon – parents should regard this as natural behaviour in children between the ages of six months and two years (and, in rare cases, even up to the age of four).

These movements help children relax and go to sleep, just as they become sleepy in a car or by being swung to and fro in a hammock.

Other repetitive actions

In this category belongs a large group of complicated monotonous actions generally made by the mouth or the area around the mouth. For babies, they are not only a means of relieving tension and boredom, but also a source of oral pleasure and satisfaction. They are more likely than monotonous movement to occur during the day, but they do become more frequent towards bedtime. As with those already mentioned, these actions should not be regarded as 'bad' or – God forbid – evidence of a psychological disorder. Only very rarely, when they are particularly frequent or intense, do they interfere with children's normal activities or endanger their health. In such cases, you should consult your doctor, and it is also advisable to do so if such phenomena appear suddenly when children are older.

To this group belong: nail biting; teeth grinding; pulling out hair, and playing with hair in all sorts of ways, such as curling it round a finger, chewing it and so on. (The damage done to the child's hair is temporary and the bare spots which may appear as a result of hair being pulled out – they really can't be called 'bald patches' – are soon covered with new hair.) The following should also be included in this group: self-inflicted scratches on the face, sucking a pillow case or sheet and, of course, fingersucking of all sorts (thumbsucking, stroking the nose with a finger, sucking a lock of hair into a curl, sucking the index or middle finger).

I do not recommend that you stop these actions, and you certainly should not attempt any 'folk' remedies such as smearing your child's finger with something bitter tasting, tying it up in a cheesecloth bandage or the like. *Up to the age of six or seven (when the adult teeth begin to appear), thumbsucking does no lasting damage to the teeth.*

Problems of separation with two-year-olds

At this age, children find that going to sleep means a temporary separation from their whole family and from all their possessions – in fact, from their whole world – and not just from their parents as was the case at the end of their first year.

Most children up to this age (though by no means all) have no difficulty whatsoever with sleeping or going to sleep. A few do suffer from problems which have to do with lack of sleep, difficulty in going to sleep, or persistent crying. However, from the second year onwards, a great majority of all children find that going to sleep starts to be a difficult problem. Parents who have not been forewarned of this tend to harbour fears that their children are abnormal or to be afraid that their childrearing methods may have been flawed. Sometimes the problem becomes so acute that even parents who have been forewarned find it hard to believe that their children's behaviour is still quite normal.

Naturally, uncertainty can only exacerbate the problem. At this age, difficulties with going to sleep originate, again, in the fear of separation. Two-year-old children are afraid of being left alone in the dark while the everyday routine of the whole family continues without them. They are afraid of having to abandon everything – their parents whom they love more than anything else, the world that is pulsing with activity – to be surrounded instead by darkness and the unknown. At bottom, their fear is of being abandoned by everyone and everything during the night and not finding anything left of their familiar environment the next morning.

These problems usually begin fairly suddenly, without warning, rather than gradually, and they come fully developed. One evening, after children have been put to bed, the problems are suddenly there. After receiving their goodnight kiss, children suddenly want a glass of water or another goodnight kiss, or need to use the potty, or have a sudden, urgent desire to blow their nose, or their teddy bear has fallen out of bed, or creases in the sheet are making them uncomfortable, etc., etc.

Each of these individual wants may be quite reasonable and the parent on duty complies with it. Sooner or later, however, the moment comes to make clear to children that 'This is the last request. I don't want to hear any more after this!' The snag is that the number of 'last requests' changes and increases from one night to the next, and that the 'last request' is very seldom really the last one.

It is very hard to find a solution that will satisfy everyone in this situation, but it is important to recognize the problem and treat it with all the care it deserves. You will certainly be able to cope with it better if your confidence is not undermined by fears or doubts that your child may be 'not quite healthy' or 'not quite right'. You must grasp the fact that the problem is rooted in your child's fear of separation and his or her attempts to win time. Once you have understood that, you can leave everything else to healthy common sense, and your natural parental instinct.

Here is one more piece of advice for parents: they should set a limit to the time they spend with their children, one that the children will normally agree to in advance. For example, put on a record or cassette for them and promise that you will stay in the room until the music is finished. Even a one-and-a-half-year-old can understand that sort of time limit. Then: goodnight!

But what is to be done if all methods fail and you are really on the brink of despair? What if your child persistently and obstinately makes exaggerated demands which go beyond what patience can endure?

For this situation I would like to suggest an additional remedy. But I must make it clear that it should only be used as a last resort: have someone else to put your child to bed. You can ask a relative – the child's grandmother, for example, or a favourite aunt. You can also entrust your child to an experienced babysitter while you leave the house specially for the purpose. This will possibly make the child less demanding.

Saying goodnight: the going-to-bed rituals of two-and-a-half-year-olds

This age is usually characterized by children's desire for consistency and a stable environment: a familiar world that does not change much, the same person to bring them up and care for them, and a uniform daily routine. Compare a child of this age with someone crossing a bridge over an abyss. Provided the bridge has a rail on each side, there is no difficulty, but if there are no rails to give a sense of security, the crossing will be very difficult. The security afforded by the rails represents the security that familiar surroundings give the child. Of course it does not mean that the child has lost his or her fear of separation, which in fact reaches its peak at the age of two. It only means that this fear has diminished a little and that it is now accompanied by a 'ritual' factor.

Children's need for unchanging circumstances and a familiar, recurring ritual before going to sleep begins before their parents are even aware of it. They usually first discover it when their children demand all sorts of things, sometimes strange things, before going to sleep, and repeat these demands every evening. It is as well for parents to recognize this phenomenon from the start and put a stop to it before it grows into a deep-rooted habit that will influence badly the child's ability to go to sleep, which at a later stage may even jeopardize his or her chance of going to sleep altogether.

As time goes on, children, if allowed, will perfect and elaborate on their bedtime rituals, turning them into full-blown cults. It can be amazing to see the degree of precision that children will insist on in every detail, and the extent to which the whole family's night can be ruined by the slightest deviation from the exact uniformity they want to achieve. The same sequence of events must be meticulously observed every time. It may begin with all the members of the family wishing the child 'goodnight'; even the way these two words are spoken and the number of kisses the child receives. A rigidly adhered to sequence of events indicates the child's desire for order. I have known of cases where, before going to sleep in the evening, children arranged dozens of dolls and pictures in a particular order beside their beds.

Many parents have to tell their children exactly the same stories every evening or play them exactly the same music, and this prelude to sleep has to be repeated with monotonous regularity every night. Parents must be careful, however, not to let the ritual get longer and longer. If just once fond parents, feeling good humoured and indulgent, read their children an extra story or play another record, they will have fallen into the trap: from that point on, as long as the thirst for ritual lasts, they will have to listen to the same demands from their two-and-a-half-year-olds in the same order every evening. Before the parents have time to realize it, their children can develop a ritually determined habit that is intertwined with going to sleep. The possibilities are endless!

I am sure that parents who are warned in time will understand the need to forestall the development of a complicated ritual which threatens to be repeated night after night.

Children's yearning for their mothers

This phenomenon usually emerges in children of two-and-a-half to three-and-a-half years old. They not only want desperately to be put to bed by their mothers, but they want them to stay with them all the time and even get into bed with them until they fall asleep. If these demands are not met, the children become increasingly difficult to get to sleep. This desire for their mothers is apparently something imperative for children of this age, and you should not be afraid that they will become too spoiled if you give in to them or that they will develop any complexes (such as the Oedipal one). It is best to accede to some of the demands of these children since the closeness they desire is vitally necessary for them and helps them in the difficult business of having to part from a world throbbing with life and go to sleep alone in the dark. So try to summon up all your patience and set aside enough time to stay with them, whenever possible, until they go to sleep. Be patient, and give them a lasting sense of security. It is also a very good idea to put a favourite doll into bed with them to serve as a contact with the outside world.

On the other hand, the following rules should be kept to without compromise: parents should never get into bed with their children, and they should not under any circumstances take their children out of bed. Children's beds must be places that provide them with a sense of security, so they should be encouraged to stay in them by parents remaining nearby. Children must never feel that they are being abandoned when they go to sleep.

Parents should also avoid giving any opportunity for ineradicable habits to form. However, during this period – and only this period – they may stay a little longer with their children to soothe and encourage them, but they must take care to leave the room before they fall asleep, to allow them *to go to sleep on their own*.

Three-year-olds: waking in the night, sleepwalking and talking

While difficulties about going to sleep gradually pass, in their place new problems appear. Completely normal and healthy children, who, up until now, may have found it hard to go to sleep but have been able to overcome this, suddenly find it difficult to sleep right through the night. They wake up once or perhaps several times for different lengths of time. Many lie quietly in bed and then fall asleep again; others play in their rooms by themselves for a couple of hours, happy with their own company, and then go calmly and contentedly back to bed.

However, it can also happen that children take to what is medically called *somnambulism*: they climb out of bed and walk around in their sleep, sometimes without making a sound, sometimes talking loudly to themselves. Some of these sleepwalking children go into the lavatory or the kitchen, and are sometimes found sleeping in the living room the next morning. A few even go so far as to leave the house and wander around outside. Occasionally children go into their parents' room, stand by their bed and look at them wide-eyed, without seeming to see them. It is as though they are looking 'through' a transparent image of their parents, without actually perceiving them.

It is very hard to know what state these children are in as they wander around like this: are they asleep, or are they in a dazed half-sleep or are they wide awake? The expressions on their faces give no reliable clues: closed eyelids are certainly always a sign that a child is asleep; but open eyes are no absolute proof to the contrary. The greatest danger of accidents happening arises when children are in an in-between state of hazy consciousness. Children who are fully awake or fully asleep are usually in no danger. Even in the intermediate state of half-sleep, they are usually capable of avoiding obstacles in their way. In a situation like this, parents are well advised to make sure that all exits from the house and all unbarred windows are kept shut and locked. They should also be careful to put away securely anything dangerous.

While it is certainly true that children are usually able to take care of themselves and avoid obstacles on their nightly expeditions, this is a far remove from the fairy tales and mystical notions which claim that sleepwalking children are able to walk along the windowsills of high buildings or perform other daredevil acts without hurting themselves. There are absolutely no grounds for such claims. Children can take care of themselves to a certain extent, but there are limits to their prudence. Possibly there have been cases in which children have carried out dangerous exploits in their sleep, but their sense of balance, judgement, discretion and so on are certainly not at their most acute in this state. As a matter of fact, there have been many accidents in which sleepwalking children have come to harm. So parents should take good care of sleepwalking children and not rely on their instinct.

All the same, do not got too far with your precautions. Admittedly, this activity can take parents by surprise and be very worrying. Many people even class this strange wandering as a psychological illness, or regard such children warily and call them 'moonstruck'. But once parents have recognized the phenomenon, they can do something to combat it.

Instead of making things difficult for these children, their mothers and fathers should let them do what they like, and make it easy for them. For example, make it simple for children to reach a light switch so that they can put it on in the middle of the night. If parents do this, they can be sure that this period of wandering in the night will be short lived. Sometimes it even passes so quickly that parents are never aware of it having happened.

If children do wake up and get out of bed, parents should look after them *from a distance*. If the nocturnal walk proceeds uninterrupted and they return to bed, parents should not try to help. They also must not wake their sleepwalking children! If parents absolutely insist, they can give their children the minimum amount of help necessary, turning them in the direction of their beds, for example, and later, when they have got back into bed, covering them up. Careful help of this sort will do no harm; the children will be neither spoiled nor encouraged to develop bad habits. In any case, they will not remember anything the next morning. Of course if parents do the opposite – lock their children's bedroom doors, set an alarm so that they wake up when the children do and then take them back to bed forcibly – things will just be made more difficult for everyone, and it will take the children longer to get over this aberration, which may then degenerate into a full-blown problem.

One more important point: under no circumstances should children be asked questions or probed about their nightly activities, nor should parents try to discuss this with them. Parents who do so only want to satisfy their own curiosity, while possibly causing their children great worry. Unless they are told about what they did the night before, they will not remember anything about it and will not think they have been involved in anything unusual. Parents' questions and reactions may give them the impression that they have done something wrong, something of which they are not aware, and over which they have no control, and which could be dangerous. The combination of parents' curiosity and concern about things their children have apparently done but of which the children are unaware may engender fears and anxieties about the unknown. That in turn may result in more serious and more frequent acts of somnambulism.

This phenomenon should be seen as a stage in the development of the sleeping process and as altogether normal. It begins during the last phase of deepest sleep and has nothing to do with dreaming. At a very early age, babies may sometimes cry and howl and parents and others think this is because they are having a bad dream. However, specialists who have investigated the sleeping process and the phenomena that accompany it are convinced that this sort of thing occurs during the final phase of deepest sleep and is in no way connected with the dreaming phase. They believe that it happens because the children cannot move on from this deep sleep to the next phase, the first of a new sleep cycle. Therefore, they wake up only partially and perform these actions in their sleep.

Whatever its cause, it is certainly true that *sleepwalking is a normal phenomenon* which has nothing to do with children's psychological states and cannot influence them in the future. Rest assured that if children mutter incoherently in their sleep, they are not giving away any 'hidden secrets'. It is advisable, therefore, to ignore the phenomenon and not to draw any conclusions from it about your children's mental condition.

Excessive tiredness can make the condition worse, so it is a good idea to let children sleep for a few hours longer during the day, if that is possible, and they should be put to bed earlier in the evening, too. But parents should not be disappointed if even this has no effect on their children. It is important to realize that it is not a question of nocturnal fears or nightmares, but just a phenomenon of infantile sleep and quite normal in young children.

Nocturnal anxiety

This is a rare additional phenomenon which belongs to the category of rhythmic movements. It is less common than children's fear of separation from their mothers but it is nevertheless one of the *normal* phenomena associated with sleeping and going to sleep. It is absolutely clear that nocturnal anxiety is not a sign of illness and there are no grounds for fearing it might damage children's health, even if it seems very worrying to parents and even outside observers. It may be that it is a necessary phase in many children's development – a natural reaction to tension and psychological anxieties, a sort of safety valve which allows feelings to escape while children are asleep, ensuring that they will be able to function properly the next morning.

The age at which nocturnal anxiety appears varies between two-and-a-half and seven, but it occurs most frequently between five and five-and-a-half. As far as the form it takes is concerned, its intensity, the contributory factors, the correct treatment and prognosis, it can be classified with the anxiety which appears before and after the age of six.

Before that age, the fears correspond perfectly to children's expanding world. To begin with, they make their appearance in the bed, then under or near the bed, and finally can be found anywhere in children's rooms.

The intensity of dreams and children's reaction to them also change as they grow. When children are between one-and-a-half and three, fear of the dark can develop and may even continue, compounded by new fears, when they are older. By this age, children are able to tell us that they have been dreaming. Sometimes dreams will wake children up. It is not common for them to wake screaming, because their dreams are not particularly terrifying at this age, and they calm down again quickly. At the age of three-and-a-half children may be afraid of bugs or other pests which they think are in their beds. At five-and-a-half, the age at which children are most susceptible to such phenomena, some are afraid of wild animals, created by their imaginations, and they also fall prey to frightening dreams and nightmares as well as to nocturnal anxiety. As a result, both children and their parents can become worried about this so that real fears, worries and difficulties set in.

A small proportion of six-year-olds, mostly girls, are afraid of 'baddies' under the bed. At seven, fears centre on shadows and objects in the room which children take for evil ghosts; or they may be afraid that robbers have slipped into the house and are hidden in a cupboard.

Frightening dreams and nightmares in children up to the age of six

Frightening dreams and nightmares are fundamentally different from each other, even though they may appear similar in the way they occur. Frightening dreams are not a lesser form of nightmare. They are what their name suggests: frightening visions which appear in dreams, whose evil portent makes dreamers wake up in panic to seek help. After waking, it will take children some time to calm down and it may be hard for them to go to sleep again. They have woken up completely and the dreams usually remain imprinted on their memories.

Nightmares, on the other hand, have nothing to do with dreams. Like somnambulism, they occur during the deepest stage of sleep or, to be more exact, during the fourth phase of peaceful sleep. When children have nightmares, they 'wake' with a cry of fright, their breathing is deep and irregular, they sweat, their pupils are dilated and they look straight ahead with their eyes open and fear is reflected in their faces. However, this facial expression is not associated with anything frightening, it is not the result of a dream, nor is it prompted by any feeling. In this state, children sit up in bed or run around and seize hold of some piece of furniture or someone in the room. Since they are not fully conscious it is no use trying to calm them. It is also very difficult to help them back to reality. The episode generally lasts about 15 minutes and *ends quite abruptly*. Immediately afterwards, children go back to bed and peacefully resume their sleep with no memory of what has happened.

A frightening dream is much less dramatic. The episode lasts only a minute or two. It begins with a sharp cry and a jerk of the body. Children wake up without sweating and fully conscious, recognizing their surroundings. They chat a little and tell what they have seen in their dreams. Only after considerable difficulty do they go back to bed and resume their sleep.

With nightmares, the sleep phases are disturbed, particularly the phase where the sleeper momentarily wakes up.

During nightmares, children are half awake but unable to wake up completely. In some cases, they may walk in their sleep as well. Nightmares occur at the point of transition from the deepest sleep to a new sleeping cycle. This means that they have nothing to do with dreams, so it is not surprising that children do not remember the dreams that supposedly woke them up.

With frightening dreams, not only are the sleeping phases disturbed but also the process of going to sleep. After waking because a dream has frightened them, children are fully conscious, and so it takes them a considerable time to calm down and go back to sleep.

These differences are very important when it comes to dealing with the problem. With nightmares, children seem to be in a state of extreme fear, but do not usually wake up, and once this state has passed, they go back to bed and remember nothing about it. (A good many children, however, develop a fear of going to sleep without even knowing what they are afraid of.) Parents should try not to wake their children as long as their semi-conscious state does not put them in any danger. The children will usually calm down of their own accord and go back to bed. If they are woken, this can frighten them. They suddenly find themselves in an unnatural situation, possibly in surroundings they cannot account for, not knowing how they got there. They will naturally feel that something terrible has happened to them, something which they were not aware of and over which they had no control.

With frightening dreams and run-of-the-mill 'bad' dreams, however, children wake up completely and are usually able to give their parents an account of the unpleasant dream. In this case, children need the encouragement of their parents, who should calm them and give them self-confidence. Children will go to sleep only after their parents have made lengthy efforts to reassure them.

All these sleep phenomena are, as I have said, very rare, and they occur in *normal* healthy children. If parents know how to handle them correctly, they will disappear in a short time. After making sure that they are genuine fears and not some performance that the children put on to attract their attention, parents should take them very seriously even if they seem silly and illogical. Always remember that the children are in distress and relying more than ever upon their parents' help, closeness and understanding. Do not treat the fears lightly, and never try to talk children out of it with remarks like 'Nonsense!' or 'There's no reason to be afraid!' or 'You should be ashamed of being frightened of something like that!' and so on. If you do that, children will feel that they have been abandoned to their fears and left defenceless by parents who do not understand and are not prepared to help. That can only make their distress worse and force them to try and pretend that they are not afraid.

Now a piece of practical advice: if children are afflicted by such fears, nightmares and dreams when very young, and perhaps even later on, it is a good plan to leave a light switched on that the children can see from their beds. Just as good are small nightlights near the bed which the children can easily switch on themselves.

When children are very young, parents should also stay with them as long as possible, talking to them and assuring them of their support by their physical and psychological closeness. Children do not need lengthy explanations and will be completely contented by having their parents nearby. It is, of course, futile to try to convince them that it was all only a dream, because they are still incapable of distinguishing dreams from reality. In their world of limited ideas, the dream is still an unknown quantity; parents have to understand this and treat dream-fed fears exactly as they would real fears which have gripped their children. Love, nearness, a feeling of security, a spirit of cooperation – all are very beneficial and help children overcome their fear. Sometimes they find the solution for themselves. They might simply jump quickly back into bed so that 'the bad man under the bed' won't catch them; some children shake their heads violently to get rid of the 'bad thoughts' before they go back to sleep again.

You can help older children by, for example, 'chasing' bugs out of their bed with a sweep of your hand or by shaking the sheets or chasing 'bad spirits' out of a cupboard with a suitable gesture. In other words, *do not try under any circumstances to convince children that their fears only exist in their imagination. Behave, instead, as if you accepted the children's logic at face value.*

In more extreme cases, when nocturnal fears appear far too often – more than once in the same night, for example – and become increasingly powerful, and if the measures described above do not prove effective, parents should alter tack immediately the following day, joining forces with their children to tackle the problem. For example, if a one-year-old is afraid of being separated from his parents, you should distract him with a game of peep-bo, alternately hiding and uncovering your face: *Peep . . . bo . . . Peep . . . bo,* and so on.

If a two-year-old experiences nocturnal fears while being potty trained (even when she is making good progress and perhaps just when progress is particularly satisfactory), you should intervene to try and prevent these fears by buying her a nice new potty, painting it in lovely bright colours and decorating it with flowers. You should even allow the child to play with her own faeces.

From the age of three, it is a good idea to explain to children what sleep is, why we have to sleep, what darkness means, how the sun goes down and so on. Parents should explain it in simple language but not in too childish a way and without using comparisons that could worry them. They must emphasize, of course, that the sun goes down in the evening and comes up again in the morning and that then there will be daylight again. They can also use books written specially for children, but always remember that children are fond of hearing the same story over and over again, until their parents are thoroughly fed up.

Nightmares in children of six and up

Once children reach the age of six, nocturnal anxiety, frightening dreams and nightmares usually disappear. However, on no account should the age of six be seen as a sharp dividing line when dealing with nightmares. If nightmares do occur at this age, parents should take them seriously and even consider medical treatment.

If children have passed their sixth birthday and the attacks of sleepwalking or nightmares which began at an earlier age still persist, or are getting worse, or reappear after a period of respite, then possibly it is because the sleepwalking and/or nightmares have become psychologically conditioned. However, even in such cases there is no question of psychological or severe emotional problems and there is no cause whatsoever for alarm. In most instances, the problem has an emotional rather than a psychological basis – a matter of strong feelings which the children cannot discharge during the day and which they have suppressed because they found them difficult to cope with, feelings such as envy, fear and hatred.

In order to understand how these feelings can influence sleep and conjure up frightening dreams and nightmares, picture the following situations. Suppose, for example, that you have been shut up in a dissecting room during an anatomy lesson, or that you have visited an old cemetery or a dark cave about which gruesome tales are told. Imagine yourself in the grip of a Hitchcock thriller or detective novel, when suddenly someone grabs you from behind, or a sudden deafening crash makes you jump. It is obvious that any disturbance of this sort can give you a terrible fright; you imagine that you are being dragged backwards into an abyss by the mysterious hand of a corpse or by evil spirits, or you think the enemy or the murderer from the film has become real. Remember that children who have nightmares go to sleep with taut nerves, feeling afraid and insecure. When they wake up for a brief moment, they are already predisposed to be afraid by these initial feelings, all the more so since sleep has robbed them of all the defence mechanisms which help them to bring these feelings under control while they are awake.

Now you understand why children have nightmares about their fears. But why do they also leap out of bed during the night?

Imagine that you are in a highly tense state of alertness, ready to wake up at the least sound your baby makes during the night, or at the tiniest noise made by a thief, or that you are on a camping holiday, sleeping in a tent in a forest full of wild animals, or that you are staying in a hotel, with your money hidden under your pillow. In such situations you will be inclined to be wake at the slightest noise. You may then even wake up with a start several times during the night without even having heard a noise, the fear and anticipation you felt before going to sleep being enough to wake you repeatedly.

Frightening dreams, bad dreams, talking or crying out in one's sleep and sleepwalking can occur at any age, even in adults, and such things are usually associated with being very tired and tense. They are not real problems on their own. However, they can give rise to concern when they are very intense and occur frequently. If children over the age of six or seven have nightmares more than once a month which are also very violent, then a doctor should be consulted. As I said, we are not talking here about *isolated* cases of children talking or crying out in their sleep – that can happen to anyone – but about a frequently recurring phenomenon.

In most cases, the advice contained in this chapter will be enough to enable you to overcome the problem. In severe cases, however, medical treatment over a long period may be required. Sometimes it is a good idea for the child to undergo psychiatric treatment for the underlying problem which has caused the phenomenon. The problematic cases are those which appear in later childhood. If the child is over six, and if the parents cannot overcome the problem by the usual means, they should get specialist advice.

Waking too early

Here we are not talking about children waking up slightly early because they need less sleep, but about those waking up *very* early, with the first light of dawn. I am sure we can all remember days from our childhood when we woke up at 4.00 in the morning because of our feelings of anticipation about an outing or some other happy event, or perhaps in expectation of a day full of duties and worries. Just as familiar and as frequent is the phenomenon of the adult getting up at first light, looking out of the window to see what the weather is like, glancing at the clock, going to the lavatory, having something to drink and then going back to bed and to sleep again. Waking up early occasionally and waking up and then going back to sleep again do not constitute sleep disorders. Here we are talking about a child, or adult, who wakes up early in the morning in spite of being tired, and would gladly go back to sleep again but is unable to. Of course, this situation must persist for some time before it can be classed as a disorder.

The reason we wake in the morning and then go back to sleep is that, at or before dawn, our sleep is superficial. At such an early hour, we can be wakened by the slightest noise: rubbish collection, the first rays of the sun, the gentle hum of the fridge's motor. While we are deeply asleep during the night, noises such as these would not disturb us. Sometimes waking at crack of dawn is not even caused by noise. We wake briefly from our superficial sleep and are then able to resume sleeping quite normally. The question of a disorder arises only when we are not able to go to sleep again because of some psychological condition such as tension, worry or inner conflict – in other words, when our superficial sleep does not outweigh our inner tension.

The *occasional* waking of children, unlike adults, is usually caused by excitement about a forthcoming treat such as a birthday, a party or a school outing. To their parents' dismay, they not only wake up early in the morning but are noisy and boisterous and usually also want to let their parents share in their exuberant joy. *Occasional* early waking is not classed as a disorder. *Continual* early waking, on the other hand, is.

The probable causes of continual early waking are:

- The children do not need any more sleep.
- The children are distressed or depressed about problems from the day before that they have not been able to resolve. They then bottle these problems up until the early hours of the morning. Then, when their sleep is no longer deep enough, they wake up and cannot get back to sleep.
- Conflicts with parents or with teachers or even school-

mates can cause psychological unrest, which may wake children up in the early hours of the morning.

Many of the children who constantly wake in the early morning stay lying quietly in bed until it is time to get up. They occupy themselves with thinking or brooding, or they use the time more productively by doing homework, or going over material for their lessons that day at school. Children who are not up to such *intellectual* activity at the crack of dawn may amuse themselves by reading books. If this is the case, parents should restrict them to boring books, or at least books which will not stimulate them. Then they might be able to go back to sleep. This method may also release tension after a certain time. Sometimes doing a jigsaw puzzle will solve the problem. Like many other problems, this one will usually resolve itself of its own accord. It does not call for medical intervention unless it assumes exaggerated proportions and interferes with the child's everyday activities. Advice about how to act if it does become particularly difficult and troublesome is to be found in the next chapter.

Problems in older children

Problems with going to bed are common in children between the ages of 8 and 12. These do not constitute true sleep problems, however; instead, there are difficulties about general behaviour as children approach adolescence.

Among the behavioural problems appearing in children of this age are obstinacy, negativity, derision and rejection of the values and convictions of their parents. With adolescent children, the deliberate neglect of duty also becomes an issue; they resist the customary discipline imposed on them, wanting to adopt an original lifestyle and prove to their parents that they know better. So, just as they are recalcitrant in other respects, they also refuse to comply with their parents' wishes when it comes to going to sleep. This is not a sleep problem but a problem of negativity: children refuse to go to sleep because their parents demand that they do so.

Still later, the main problem is getting teenagers to wake up in the morning, although this can begin in younger children. Although there are always exceptions, including natural early risers, most teenagers love to sleep in. They feel tired and think they need extra sleep, even though they have already slept long enough during the night.

5

Sleep disorders requiring treatment

Children, as you know, need a long time to compose themselves before going to sleep, and this time can be greatly prolonged depending on the circumstances. For example, guests in the house can contribute to an unfamiliar atmosphere and delay children's going to sleep. Every deviation from the normal, familiar and consistent environment causes similar difficulties. Exhilarating activity before sleep is a sure recipe for problems.

It is possible to proceed from the premise that all 'sleeping difficulties' are really only a matter of definition. If parents make it easy for their children to sleep only whenever *they* feel like it, it can rightly be assumed that these parents will not be confronted with any sleeping difficulties! While this is true, there are nevertheless certain limitations to be borne in mind.

It may well be that children simply do not have any sleeping problems at this stage, since, after all, they go to sleep when it suits them. For children to have difficulties, they must find themselves in the situations where they *want* to sleep but *can't*. Later on, children will reach a stage when they have social duties (nursery and primary school) which impose a fixed timetable on them, and it is at this point that they may develop sleeping problems. The habit of going to sleep late and getting up late cannot be indulged any longer. Moreover, children do not know and cannot tell where to draw the line: if they are allowed to play until late at night, turning the house upside down or sitting glued to the television, they may forget everything else – eating, drinking, sleeping – out of sheer absorption in what they are doing or watching, only to find themselves, at a still later stage, overly tired or in such a state of excitement that it is difficult for them to get to sleep. As I have mentioned, children have many wishes and aspirations. If you know how to satisfy them, many of the problems which arise will be easily over-come. But in cases such as the one above, too lenient a parental hand, pandering to children and letting them have their own way, is only likely to implant in them the seeds of habits which will later cause great difficulties about sleep and behaviour. Sometimes the Biblical caveat is really true: Spare the rod and spoil the child.

Obviously I cannot come up with any magic formula; you simply have to understand your child's normal sleep requirements and the natural course that his or her sleep habits will take. You have to recognize the dangers to which the wrong habits will expose him or her and exploit your child's reactions according to his or her needs. How do you do this? On the one hand, by being mindful of his or her natural wishes and needs, and on the other, by not being too considerate and indulgent when to do so may lead to habits which could have a harmful effect on his or her normal development.

When you encounter sleeping problems in your children, you should always ask yourselves the following questions:

- When did you first notice the problem? You will often be able to trace the start of a problem to a particular event – an illness, for example, or an outing, the birth of another child or moving into a new house. You may also be able to put it down to a normal sleeping problem typical of a certain age. To be able to judge this, you should re-read the previous chapters.
- When the problem first appeared, how did your initial attempts to combat it work to the child's advantage? What satisfaction did he/she derive from your wish to solve his/her new problem? Did you take him/her out of bed? Did you take him/her into your own bed? Did you let him/her play with you or watch television? Did you give him/her something to eat while playing happily with you?

- What advantage does the child now get from not going to bed at the right time? What 'profit' does he/she reap from the sleeping problem? What 'reward' does he/she get to go back to sleep again?
- Could it not be that your child in fact is sleeping normally and you have simply misjudged the situation?
- Is your child's environment quiet and peaceful enough? Do his/her surroundings allow him/her to sleep undisturbed? Is he/she perhaps being disturbed by too much light or too much darkness, the temperature of the room, noise, etc.?
- Is your child in a calm enough state of mind before he/she goes to bed? Is he/she tired enough?
- Are you consistent enough in your reaction to the way he/she sleeps?
- Do you pay a lot of attention to your child in the evening, which he/she may perhaps miss during the day? For example, does he/she only see one of his/her parents in the evening when the latter comes home from work?
- Does your child have a genuinely difficult problem with waking up or going to sleep? Does he/she suffer real fears? Might his/her resistance to going to sleep be motivated by his/her fear of being parted from his/her mother or father? Or could it be that he/she just wants you to keep on making a fuss of him/her?

If these questions have not helped you to identify the source of the problem or if you have not found the answer among the 'normal' disturbances for the relevant age group, read on.

'Normal' vs. 'pathological' sleep disorders

Until now, I have been concerned with *normal* sleep in its various forms, and I have tried to instruct and advise confused and hesitant parents about how they can come to terms with sleep disorders and difficulties. I have also mentioned typical sleep disorders for each respective age group and how they can be dealt with most easily until such time as they disappear of their own accord.

Parents have to distinguish between 'normal' and 'pathological' disorders. This division is not absolute and the two respective conditions are not even uniformly described in the specialist medical literature. Normal sleep problems cease spontaneously as the child grows older, but pathological ones require treatment, not always radical treatment, but at least enough to eliminate the disturbing factor. A normal sleep problem may also become entrenched and turn into a pathological disorder.

Pathological problems in children fall into one of three groups:

1 Sleep disorders that are the result of an emotional upset.
2 Sleep disorders resulting from bad habits.
3 Sleep disorders caused by psychological illness.

Sleep disorders: reactions to emotional upset

This is the largest group among adults, and in most cases, their disorders are not pathologically conditioned but are an expression of the perfectly normal reaction of people in the grip of powerful, violent states of mind, such as tension, fear, joy, anger, disappointment, defeat, unrealized expectations and so on.

In children, examples of this might be fear of nursery school, hatred or fear of the nursery school nurse or teacher, fear of school exams, anger and disappointment at lack of sympathy from a parent or teacher or from friends or the children's social group whose fellow feeling is important to them. To this category also belong fear and regret at the anger of a parent or teacher, tension as a result of being caught out in some small dishonesty, such as failing to do homework or the like. Or it might be the children's fear of being separated from their parents or shame and embarrassment at having witnessed a violent quarrel between them.

People can bear only so much emotional pain, but the amount of this differs with each individual. It can be astonishing sometimes to see how something that is important and significant to us adults is accepted by children with indifference, while something which appears to be of no importance can cause the same children the severest sleep disorders. These same children can also react differently at different times to one and the same event. We just have to learn to recognize and allow for individual differences in personality, character, sensitivity and so on.

To this group of sleep disorders also belong children's sleeping difficulties that stem from hurt feelings, caused by thinking that their relationships with their parents have deteriorated and are not as warm as they used to be. Generally there are logical reasons why the relationship between parent and child might have changed, but sometimes these changes are only a product of children's imaginations. One situation in which hurt feelings can often arise is the new family atmosphere which accompanies the birth of a brother or sister, or a change in one of the parent's jobs, such as a move to a new place of work, or the mother going out to work for the first time in a child's life and, as a result, no longer able to devote so much time to the child at home. In most cases of this sort, children react by developing sleep problems, often without anyone being aware of the reason. The parents frequently then complain that their children are afraid to sleep in case they 'miss something'. The children, on the other hand, account for their fear of going to sleep by saying they are afraid of not waking up, of being forgotten and having to stay at home alone and abandoned.

In these cases, it is not the symptoms of the sleep disorder that should be treated but the cause – in other words, the psychological condition which has led to it. Parents should understand the root of the problem and then draw the necessary conclusions for themselves. It is generally during the day that the problem originates and so treatment is also a matter for the daytime. Parents should take care to give their children their full attention during the day. For example they should explain to them, and get them used to the idea, that one of the parents spends the day away from home at work, but comes back again in the evening. If there has been an addition to the family, older children should be allowed to help look after the new babies.

An excellent solution, and one that has proved effective in many cases, is to put the new little brother or sister to sleep in the same room as the big brother or sister. This may seem paradoxical to many parents, but the fact is that the arrangement usually works! Just try it for a few weeks and you will be able to see for yourselves. It may also help ease the hours before the older child is put to bed.

Remember that these pre-bedtime hours are the most difficult of the day: fathers come home from work tired, wanting to relax and perhaps give their partners an account of their day. Mothers have had a long day of housework or at their jobs. Both parents now face the task of putting their children to bed. Even though this can involve considerable difficulty, parents must try their utmost to approach it patiently even if they do not feel up to it. They must make convincingly clear to their children that they love them more than anything else but that the time has come to go to sleep. They must tell them that they will be back at their bedside the next morning. They can also distract their children by reading aloud to them. The content is not always important: what matters is the way the words are spoken, the soft reassuring style of reading and the loving bond between parents and children which this communicates. Even a baby of one-and-a-half can 'understand' and 'enjoy' stories read in this way.

Sleep disorders resulting from bad habits

The most frequent cause of all pathological problems is that *sleep has become conditional on some other factor.*

Babies and toddlers have to learn to go to sleep of their own accord without help from other people, not even from their parents. Sometimes parents think that the easiest way of overcoming a particular sleeping problem is to make some concession to their babies. Many parents, for example, are prepared to give their children a bottle before they sleep or to take them into their own bed – simply so that the babies will go to sleep quickly and there will be peace in the house. Sometimes parents even enjoy singing their children to sleep, or walking them up and down until they drop off. Such practices stem from the parents' own inclinations.

Parents must remember that everything children do (or is

done to them) before they go to sleep very quickly becomes *a habit they cannot do without!*

I must stress once again that I am not talking here about a ceremony or an activity that children perform before they are put to bed, such as eating the evening meal or spending time with parents, nor about playing or having stories read to them during the evening. I am only talking about things which children do *immediately before they go to sleep.*

What is actually so bad about habits which do not endanger children or inconvenience parents? If the habit is really insignificant, such as sucking a dummy or cuddling a doll, or even having a story read to them in bed, it will do children no harm and may even be a good thing. However, if the habit is such that children can only go to sleep when, say, they have been given a bottle or they are ensconced in their parents' bed, then it can easily deteriorate into a severe problem of sleep disturbance. The reason is that these activities, which give the superficial appearance of helping the children to go to sleep, really stimulate them, making it harder for them to drop off and disturbing their sleep later on.

It is also true that, by their very nature, these habits are likely to become more acute, ramifying and spreading until they are out of control and have become very disruptive for the parents as well as the children. Babies who have acquired such a habit will become very tired and sleepy but will not be able to go to sleep until their habitual need has been appeased. The lack of this disturbs them, wakes them up and causes them distress, and they can't do anything about it. Moreover, the need to indulge in a particular habit is also likely to wake these children up repeatedly during the night and keep them awake for long periods!

Why does this happen? As we have seen, sleep is made up of cycles, each 90 minutes long. Between cycles, people wake up very briefly, change their sleeping positions, momentarily check their surroundings and fall back into the next cycle of sleep. During the process, they become aware of any changes which may have taken place in their environment from the way they remember it when they fell asleep. Babies who have got used to a certain precondition for going to sleep – being given a bottle, for example, or being in their parents' bed – cannot accept that is not happening without making a protest. The resulting disturbance makes them wake up completely, at which point they expect and demand to get whatever it is that they habitually need for going to sleep. The fact that this is not forthcoming is naturally a source of great disappointment for them, and, eventually, for their parents, too.

With children who are plagued by repeated episodes of waking at night, it will not be long before a further problem comes along. Since these children know that they will wake up during the night, they will do all they can to avoid it happening; they will try their best to put off going to sleep, and so will turn falling asleep in the evening into a problem, too. The children come to see sleeping and going to sleep as unpleasant and uncomfortable, something that makes them miserable, and they will try to ward it off by winning time with all their might.

Waking at night

The inability to sleep right through the night is a pathological sleep disorder. It is also a very common one. The root of the trouble lies precisely in bad habits associated with going to sleep – that is, in fixed preconditions for going to sleep which have become deeply rooted over the course of time. This expresses itself by children waking up several times during the night and finding it very hard to go to sleep again. I hope that the case study described here will contribute to a better understanding of the problem.

Michael was a 20-month-old boy. His parents told me:

The baby usually wakes up three times a night and cries until we go to him. Each time, he stays awake for about an hour and only goes to sleep after one of us has got into bed with him and rubbed his back for half an hour. At the same time, we have to play him music on a cassette. This procedure is repeated three times every night. In the last few days, Michael has also been finding it difficult to fall asleep in the evening. The whole family is close to a collective nervous breakdown. We no longer have the strength to go through nights like this. We have tried everything, even leaving Michael to cry, which meant that he roared for hours, so much so that we felt we had to give him what he wanted. Once, when we did not go to him, because we were both exhausted, he cried until he made himself sick. What on earth should we do?

So far, Michael's parents had not mentioned a word about the way they put him to bed, not thinking this was of any consequence. However, after I had questioned them further, Michael's mother continued:

We do not have any difficulty in putting Michael to bed. He does need a particularly long bedtime ritual, but I'm very patient and I devote a lot of time to him which I'm happy to do. Once he is in bed, I get in beside him, rub his back, and play him a song or tell him a story. This routine lasts about an hour, until my husband gets home from work . . .

When Michael wakes up during the night, I repeat the same ritual and he calms down and goes to sleep. But how can I get up three times a night and spend an hour with him each time? How much time is left for me to sleep? When Michael wakes up, he often has specific things he wants, and seems a little anxious, but he never looks really frightened.

Michael's parents then admitted that, recently, a certain deterioration had been noticeable and that their little boy had been increasingly putting off the moment for going to bed.

Now I was sure that, despite all the signs to the contrary, the root of Michael's problem lay precisely in the habitual process by which he went to sleep, not in the frequently interrupted night-time sleep itself. Michael was a perfectly normal and healthy child. He did not have any sleep problems. His only problem was that, every time he woke up, he naturally wanted to go to sleep again and had linked this need to a ritual which his parents had fostered until it had become an indispensable habit. For Michael, this habit had now become a genuine need and he had a right to satisfy it! He would go to sleep only after he had been offered what he had been led to expect.

Michael's problem is only one example of many similar ones that I have encountered. I am only going into it in detail here as an example of conditioning in general, and of trying to find a way of solving the problems of waking up in the night by seeing them in the context of difficulties with going to sleep – difficulties which in Michael's case can be wholly ascribed to conditioned habits.

As I have said, Michael was a perfectly healthy little boy who did not actually have a sleeping problem. This was confirmed by the fact that he had no trouble in going to sleep and sleeping well, provided that the circumstances to which he had become accustomed prevailed.

Michael's nightly waking was a natural and perfectly healthy phenomenon. It is essentially similar to the brief waking of any small child and of any normal person – the momentary interval of wakefulness between one sleep cycle and the next, during which we change our position and fleetingly check our surroundings. The root of Michael's problem was that he found it difficult to go to sleep again, or rather, he found it difficult to satisfy the habit which for him was inseparably bound up with going to sleep again.

Michael had become accustomed to going to sleep only in the middle of a ritual which lasted about an hour, when his mother would lie in bed beside him, rub his back and play him music or read him a story. Obviously, whenever Michael woke up in the night, he became aware of far-reaching changes in this environment and his healthy instinct ensured that he was soon wide awake. In his new circumstances, he was unable to go back to sleep. For Michael to go to sleep – in any situation – his indispensable preconditions had to be satisfied.

The solution to Michael's problem was, simply put, that he had to be broken of the habit, and had to be taught to go to sleep by himself following only a short ritual.

There are several reasons why his parents failed in their own efforts to overcome the problem, and we can draw lessons from these. The parents' basic mistake was trying to cure only their child's waking up repeatedly at night, thinking that this and only this was what they had to combat. In fact, they should have set about changing the whole way in which he went to sleep in the early evening. At first, however, the problem of his going to sleep did not seem important. His mother had plenty of time and patience, and in any case, she really enjoyed devoting an hour or so to her child before her husband came home from work. The fact that Michael had become used to a long goodnight ritual involving his mother before he could go to sleep was the root of the whole problem. It is interesting that the parents were completely unaware of the connection between their child's ritual for getting to sleep and his repeated nightly waking. For them – quite rightly from their point of view – the aim was to make the child sleep right through the night without interruption.

As the parents told me, they did try to train Michael: they let him cry and avoided entering his room. Only when they thought he had been crying for too long or when they could not bear his crying any longer did they capitulate and go in to him. In other words, the parents thought they could 'train' their child by letting him cry, not realizing that the solution was only to be found in a fundamental change in his ritual for going to sleep. This is the reason why, when Michael stopped crying, they again resorted to the usual going-to-sleep ceremony.

Michael's parents tried to tackle the problem in one go, they did not try to make any changes in the going-to-bed ritual: two fundamental mistakes. If you have a problem about nightly waking or other difficulties of this kind, the following is the right course of action.

First, *the treatment must be carried out gradually, step by step!* The second aim should be to *concentrate treatment on the going-to-bed ritual*. The repeated nightly waking should be treated less intensively and at a later stage. The crying that occurs is only a by-product, and stopping it is, therefore, not a separate goal. Obviously the fervour and duration of the crying should not be taken as a measure of the success or failure of the treatment. In no way is it the aim of the treatment to punish children, or cause them suffering and make them cry, but, nevertheless, you will have to put up with a certain amount of wailing.

The one part of the treatment that must be adhered to right from the start is the following principle: *children must learn how to go to sleep by themselves and within the framework of a ritual that is as short as possible*. This fundamental principle cannot be applied in stages and you must not compromise at all. For example, getting into bed with your child and rubbing his/her back (or similar ritualized behaviour) must stop at once and for all!

The step-by-step approach usually applies only to the length of the time that the parents allow their children to cry before going into their room. However, in particularly severe cases, parents may also have to deal with the various stages of the going-to-sleep ritual one by one. They may perhaps begin by tackling their children's need to have their mothers in bed with them and only later deal with the habit of listening to music or being told a story. But in general it is best to deal with the whole going-to-sleep ritual at once.

Day 1

- Put your child to bed and leave the room, but leave the door open. Of course, your child will burst into tears and begin to howl. You can calm him/her by speaking to him/her from outside the room, but you must not go back inside straightaway. Wait five minutes. Then go to the child, reassure him/her and impress upon him/her that he/she must go to sleep.
- After staying in the room for a minute or two, you should leave again. This time, stay out for ten minutes. After that, you should go back into the room, reassure your child as you did the first time.
- Leave again – this time for 15 minutes.

On the first day of treatment, parents should not worry if their children cry for periods of up to 15 minutes each time. The procedure should be repeated for as long as it takes the children to go to sleep.

Please note: parents should only go into their children's room to calm them very briefly – and for their own peace of mind to make sure that everything is all right. *The children must learn to go to sleep by themselves*, but they should not feel that the change of habit expected of them is a punishment. They must therefore be reassured so that they realize that their parents sympathize and are not abandoning them or ignoring them. The children will probably calm down a little and stop crying every time their parents go into the room, although stopping them crying is not the purpose of the exercise. They will probably begin to cry again as soon as their parents leave because, of course, the children then once more face the problem of going to sleep without outside assistance. Parents should continue in the same way throughout the night, although later they can make the pauses between bouts of crying a little shorter.

Day 2

You wait ten minutes before interrupting the first bout of tears (instead of the original five minutes on the first day of treatment). You then let the second bout of crying continue for 15 minutes, and after that, interrupt only every 20 minutes.

Day 3

Allow the first bout of crying to go on for 15 minutes before interrupting, the second for 20 minutes, and each subsequent one for 25 minutes.

In most cases, the problem will clear up by itself after a few days, provided that parents keep consistently to the instructions for treatment.

Promoting good sleeping habits in stages

	NUMBER OF MINUTES TO WAIT UNTIL YOU GO INTO THE CHILD'S BEDROOM TO CALM HIM/HER DOWN		
	Crying period one	*Crying period two*	*Crying period three (and each crying period thereafter)*
Day 1	5	10	15
Day 2	10	15	20
Day 3	15	20	25

Out of the hundreds of cases which I have treated, I remember only two that took more than three days. For children like this, I suggest that you allow crying to last 30 minutes before interrupting.

Children must be brought to the stage of being able to go to sleep by themselves in virtually any situation. Since this is very difficult for children and is accompanied by a lot of crying, the appearance of parents in their children's rooms (in order to interrupt each bout of crying) must be accompanied by soothing words. Parents must remember that the sole purpose of their visit is *to soothe their children*, and *not under any circumstances to send them to sleep*.

Before beginning this method of treatment, it is sensible to take the precaution of working out a timetable (such as the one on p. 117), so that you will know each day how long you should stay out of your child's room and let him or her cry and by how much to increase the interval between each interruption of the crying. It is also a good idea to use a stopwatch or electronic timer. On no account should you give in to your child's crying. In the night and under this sort of stress, when the child you love is crying heartrendingly and may even be waking the neighbours, every minute seems like an eternity, and your natural inclination will be to stop the crying before the time is up. But if you do, you run the risk of jeopardizing the whole process of treatment.

Having said this, however, it is not a good idea to stick mechanically to a strict timetable. It is always a good thing to rely on sound common sense and, to some extent, be guided by your feelings. What this means in practice is that the timetable should be designed to suit the individual needs of the child. For example, if the child has already been crying almost for the specified time, but has calmed down and is showing an inclination to go to sleep, it is best not to go into the room whatever the timetable says.

The one-stage method
It is worth mentioning that the step-by-step training method which I have described here in detail is not the only possibility. *Provided you treat the right elements of the sleep disorder – that is, the problem of going to sleep and the*

conditioned habit associated with it – and provided you follow this treatment through consistently, you may also solve the problem with the one-stage method. This has a long and successful history – for example, it was recommended by Dr Spock!

To use the one-stage method, parents should put their babies to bed, soothe them and explain to them as far as possible that they must go to sleep by themselves. Even one-and-a-half-year-old children 'understand' instinctively if they are soothed and spoken to in a tender, loving way by their parents. The parents must then wait outside the open door of their children's room and comfort them periodically from this observation post, without entering the room themselves, even if the children roar violently for hours. If they wake in the night, one of the parents goes to their bed and calms them but should not stay in the children's room. It is very important that parents should leave the room again; at most, they can stay in the next room.

In the majority of cases this method, too, will probably be crowned with success – the children simply have no other alternative. However, I must admit that the number of failures is greater than with the step-by-step method, since many parents cannot summon up the strength of mind to cope with the stress it involves.

Therefore, I prefer to recommend the step-by-step treatment, for the following reasons:

It is extremely likely that parents will be unable to see the one-stage treatment through simply because they will not be able to stand the crying of their children. Consequently they run the risk of throwing in the towel during the course of treatment, and if they do this even once, they have lost their chance of success.

The change from one extreme to the other is also likely to confuse the children. They will not understand what their parents are aiming at. They will be disconcerted by what they see as their parents' inconsistency and will be threatened by thoughts about being punished for something they are not aware of having done. They cannot understand why their mother or father rushed to their side the first time they cried during the night and helped them to go to sleep again, and now they are suddenly refusing to aid their children in their distress.

In fact, only a few parents use the one-stage, 'once and for all' method of treatment described here, and it is heartening to hear why more do not. Most parents who seek medical advice make it unequivocally clear that they have already tried the method and decided against it. 'If you are going to advise us to leave the baby to cry all night and not go near him, you'd better keep your advice to yourself,' they tell the doctor. 'It hasn't worked for us.'

Vomiting

Occasionally babies vomit because of the exertion of crying. If this happens, parents must make sure immediately that no vomit has got into their children's windpipes. It goes without saying that they should clean them up and change their night clothes.

On the other hand, parents should not see this in too tragic a light and allow their babies the satisfaction of making capital out of it. Parents must not, for example, 'compensate' their babies by becoming lax in the training procedure. Quite the contrary: they must carry on where they left off, as if nothing unusual has happened.

Parents usually have no idea what sharp hearng babies have and how ingenious they can be in attracting their mothers' and fathers' attention. This sort of vomiting does not harm babies, and parents should not reproach themselves if it happens. The same is true of persistent crying: this is part of the natural process of acquiring new habits for going to sleep. It is something that will disappear along with other associated phenomena, provided that you treat it consistently.

Breathlessness

Attacks of breathlessness or uneven breathing are not uncommon. Babies' crying, accompanied by lusty roaring, becomes louder and louder. Then, suddenly, after a loud cry or even without any advance warning, they stop breathing, go blue in the face, roll their eyes, distort their features and become unconscious. An attack like this usually lasts several moments, and, on rare occasions, it can be followed by convulsions (a 'fit'). It is a really frightening thing to happen, even for the most heroic parents, and especially the first time.

Of course, children who have had this happen must be taken to the family doctor to confirm that this was the result of prolonged crying and not a symptom of an illness. Once the doctor – and only the doctor! – has confirmed the diagnosis and ascertained that it was an attack of breathlessness, everyone can heave a sigh of relief. It is a well-known phenomenon, by no means rare and it does no damage at all to a child's health. Amazed parents may object that this is impossible – 'After all, the brain gets no supply of oxygen at times like that,' they may assert. Let me enlighten you and reassure you categorically:

An attack of breathlessness does not harm the child in the least.

An additional difficulty associated with this sort of attack is the influence it can have on the way parents interpret the whole question of sleep problems. Many parents incline to the conviction that their children's behaviour must always be natural and right, and that that is the most reliable criterion you can use. But even if we agree with the presupposition that children know best how to satisfy their needs and behave accordingly, it is still debatable what children's true needs are when they are in the middle of such an attack. The ones most likely to be affected are those who are active, periodically nervous, very dependent on their parents and extremely spoiled. If these attacks become progressively worse, and indirectly benefit the children (by the attention they receive afterwards), they usually have their origin in the children's subconsciouses.

Contrary to widespread opinion, the conclusion that must be reached is that these children need strong discipline. Their parents should devote less attention to them and be strict with them, hardening their hearts and even rejecting them a little; they should not pander to them, give in to them or try to appease them. If parents behave in exactly the opposite way during the crises, so that their children can draw indirect advantage from them, then, believe me, the attacks will get progressively stronger and worse.

So if it looks as though an attack of breathlessness has been caused by crying as a result of your strict training, you should nevertheless continue with your method undeterred and with complete conviction, despite all the difficulties. Like babies who make themselves sick, the attack is a result of crying and should cause you no more concern than violent crying which is not accompanied by such a side-effect. If you are sure that the training methods you are applying are the best and that they will not cause your child any harm but will bear fruit as you hope, you will be better able to withstand this trial. You have my promise on that.

Psychological damage

Many parents are troubled by the thought that their children might suffer psychological damage if they are left to cry too long and the parents are 'cruel' for paying no attention to their desperate cries for help. I find it really difficult to assure parents – in face of this apparently logical objection and because of the serious situation in which they find themselves – that this objection is not valid. To the best of my knowledge and with a clear conscience, I can dismiss all their fears and declare unequivocally that not only is this method quite harmless, but many precedents have proved it to be highly successful. It is widely accepted nowadays as a method of training babies and children, and, of course, it does not cause them any psychological damage. On the contrary, even if the two parties involved – the parents and the children – are not aware of their needs, at the end of the day the children will be subconsciously grateful to their parents for having helped them to teach themselves how to go to sleep and how to sleep well afterwards. They will be grateful for their parents' help in ridding them of the conditioned habit which used to make both the parents' and the children's nights hell.

The mother of a two-year-old girl told me the following:

Six months ago, I consulted a paediatrician because my daughter would not go to sleep under any circumstances. From the moment she was put to bed, she roared and cried and refused to go to sleep. She would eventually doze off, but only after I had picked her up, walked up and down the room with her, given her her bottle and distracted her with all sorts of devices – for a total of about two hours.

The doctor she consulted had been in no doubt that the woman was close to a breakdown, and to accommodate her, he prescribed tranquillizers in the form of suppositories for the little girl. Like many children's doctors, he probably did this less out of the conviction that it was the best method of treatment than in response to pressure from one of the parents; as a result, his conscience troubled him, so he chose the 'middle ground' of prescribing a minimum dose of the medicine.

A week later, the mother came to him and said that the suppositories had been no use and had even made the situation worse. This time the doctor suggested the method that I have outlined on pages 116–18. The doctor assured her that her child would come to no harm as a result; on the contrary, she would very soon learn to go to sleep by herself and so put an end to the problem.

'The doctor was right,' the mother admitted frankly at the end of her story. 'A week later the problem had disappeared.' Then she added rather shamefacedly. 'Even before I went to the doctor, I had an instinctive feeling that it would be better to let my little girl cry. But I didn't trust myself to take the responsibility. She objected so violently and persistently that I felt I couldn't trust my instinct.'

What this mother actually needed was simply to share the responsibility with the doctor. She wanted him to confirm that this was the most effective method of treatment and that she would not do her child any harm by carrying it out. 'It's a pity that the doctor did not tell me all this at the start,' was how she summed up her experience: 'This method was a real lifesaver for me.'

Without wishing to embark on an analysis of this child's problem or to try to prove why prescribing tranquillizers was a mistake, I would like to stress that, in this case, the mother only needed the doctor's confirmation to act as her instinct had prompted her. This would have helped her adopt a treatment which was easier and more effective than administering drugs.

This book does not seek to take over the function of a child's doctor. It is always advisable to consult your doctor if you are worried about your child's health or well-being.

Consistency

Consistency is the fundamental principle of every training procedure; baby and childcare are no exceptions to the rule.

'It's all very well for him to talk,' is what many parents think or say in response to specialist advice, 'but we would like to see how he would fare in our shoes.' A doctor cannot really do much more than make your difficult task easier by explanation and encouragement. He or she can only confirm that this method has been tested in any number of cases – some of them much more serious than yours – and has had all the success that was hoped for. Even that does not do it justice: the method has been positively effective beyond every expectation. But the precondition for success is that you rely on it, believe in it, keep to it consistently and precisely, without deviation, even if it takes a week or two before the first signs of a change for the better become apparent.

If you look for shortcuts or methods which are intended first and foremost to make things easier for *you*, you will soon find your resolve waver and you will become inconsistent, too strict one day, too indulgent the next. But what happens on the day after indulgence got the upper hand? Your child is even less able to take 'strict days' in his/her stride; they now seem all the 'crueller'. Children see this sudden strictness as incomprehensible and unjustified, and it destroys their expectations. They will never understand the connection between being left alone in their rooms and the aim of learning to go to sleep by themselves. Consistency is thus one of the central factors in this method of training and solving children's sleep problems.

The treatment of similar conditions

While I have given one specific example of overcoming a bad habit – waking at night – the problem and method of treatment applies to an enormously large group of cases. In all of them, it is a question of bad habits connected with going to sleep, of a process of going to sleep which depends on certain seemingly indispensable routines.

When giving in is perfectly all right

Many children are used to sleeping with a dummy in their mouths, or clasping some object. Sooner or later, the dummy will fall out of their mouths or the object out of their hands, but this does not interrupt their sleep. Generally, no problem should arise, but some babies, when they wake up fleetingly at the usual intervals between sleep cycles, sense that their circumstances have changed; these no longer correspond with the ones that obtained when they went to sleep. As soon as they become conscious of the change, they wake up and a problem has already arisen: they are now unable to go back to sleep until what was familiar is restored, and that can only happen with the parents' help.

In these cases, babies are usually satisfied if they are simply given back what they have lost – the dummy or other object – because the familiar environment which obtained before will then be restored. Parents who realize this from the start, and do not try other ways of calming their children will find that what they suffer as a result is not too much to put up with, even though they do have to get up every time their babies wake during the night to give them back the dummy or whatever they have dropped.

Parents should not be afraid that they will spoil their babies too much if they comply with their wishes in this matter. If the babies wake up during the night and cannot go to sleep again without knowing they have their accustomed object, they are not acting spoiled or being capricious but experiencing a genuine and legitimate need. And parents are not spoiling their children if they satisfy this need.

At worst, they are helping rather too much to implant a particular habit associated with going to sleep, and if subsequently they cannot put up with the inconvenience it causes, there is a danger that they may allow far more serious problems to develop in the future. Of course, in such cases they can always change their children's system for going to sleep. But generally this is only a theoretical possibility: just about all parents prefer getting up once or twice in the night to put the accustomed object back in their children's hands or mouths, rather than having to teach them proper habits for going to sleep, particularly since it is only a matter of a relatively short period in their babies' lives. After all, they are growing up and will soon be able to find the missing dummy or object by themselves without waking up completely.

The real problem is when parents do not recognize these situations in time and do not interpret them correctly, with the result that they do not know the right way to respond. For example, a baby's short intermittent waking during the night can develop into an hour-long ritual. Unfortunately I can remember all too many cases which began with the baby bursting into tears briefly during the night. In retrospect, one can say this happened because the baby's dummy was not put back into his/her mouth immediately, but all too soon, really serious habits developed: the baby had to be picked up out of bed and walked up and down the room, had to have stories read or music played to him or her, have a night feed, or to go on little 'expeditions' round the house or, in summertime, into the garden and so on.

Night feeds

The problem of nightly feeding related to waking in the night is one of the most difficult and widespread. Only a few parents know from the start how to deal with this problem. Many think the reason for it is something to do with the way their babies sleep, not, as we have learned, in their process of going to sleep. Others interpret the phenomenon as a symptom of hunger. Which one is correct? Up to what age is the night feed a legitimate need? And from what age should you start to wean your baby from his or her night feed?

As I have already mentioned several times, there are no sharp boundaries in medicine, no 'red lines' which must not be overstepped when bringing up babies. However, it is possible to state, with a high degree of probability that *as soon as babies are six months old, they no longer need a night feed.* They can sleep uninterruptedly for 12 hours without any *physical need* for food. If babies of about six months still demand food during the night, they are doing it *out of habit*, not out of hunger, and they will not suffer any damage to their health if they give up the night feed. Moreover, even three-month-old-babies need only a single night feed. If they demand more than that, it is a sign that this has become a matter of habit, not the result of any need for nourishment.

When the night feed becomes a problem, its cause is usually obvious. In a few cases, it is due to blind mother love, her urge to 'build the baby up'. More often it is because parents know that their babies can easily be silenced by a bottle or by being breast fed. They mistakenly allow themselves to be persuaded that it is a good thing in itself for their babies to take in more food, besides being convenient for them because then the babies will not wake up again during the night. So the habit of associating difficulty with going to sleep appears, and the babies wake several times during the night demanding something to eat or simply something to suck before they will go back to sleep.

Out of this habit yet more problems may develop. Babies become accustomed to eating during the night and, as a result, begin to feel hungry during the night! They wake up, not only because of the problem which troubled them when they went to sleep, but also because they are hungry. In tackling the problem of going to sleep, you also have to come to grips with this habit of eating at night, which is no less problematic.

There are other adverse factors to consider. Because babies are drinking too much, their nappies are always wet and full, a factor which can contribute considerably to their discomfort. Wind is also likely to form in the intestines with every extra night feed, and this may also increase their sense of unease.

As if all this were not reason enough to put a stop to unnecessary night feeds, there is the additional fact that sleep disorders of this sort, by their very nature, get spontaneously worse. In other words, babies who have been waking up once in the night to eat can then begin to wake up two or three more times and need food each time before being able to go to sleep again.

Treatment of this complicated problem must be taken step by step. The first must be for parents to give their babies only one meal in the night, which is always provided at the same time and for which they wake the babies up. This single night feed, which must be the last before the parents go to sleep, should be given between 10.00 and 11.00 p.m. By making and observing the rule that they are the ones who wake the babies, parents gain the following advantages:

- They are then sure that their babies do not need any food until the next morning. There are no grounds for concern about the intake of calories and other nourishment, and any immediate burst of crying or demand for food can be identified as the symptom of a conditioned habit and not of hunger.
- They will find it easier to arrange their own daily, or rather nightly, routine. After all, parents have certain rights too . . .

After introducing the regular night feed, the other stages of treatment can begin. The final goal is to stop giving the night feed (or several night feeds) altogether. Now parents have to decrease the amount of food they give their babies at every night feed. If the babies are being bottle fed, the amount of the feed should be reduced by 20 millilitres (ml) every day. If the babies are being breast fed, the length of the feed should be reduced by a minute each time. On no account should babies be allowed to go to sleep while they are feeding, even if this means that they cry. Once the original amount of food has been reduced by two-thirds, that feed can be discontinued altogether. In view of the small amount left, it is not necessary to do this in stages; it would only discourage and depress the babies.

At the same time, the intervals between night feeds, or rather between the times when the babies wake, must be increased – by half an hour a day. There are two possible ways of doing this: either the intervals are made longer and the amount of food is simultaneously reduced, or the amount of food is reduced to start with and the parents stay with their babies until they have calmed down and stopped crying. When the quantity of food has been reduced to nil, you begin the next stage of lengthening the intervals.

The whole procedure goes like this: using both methods at once, on the first day leave the baby to cry for an hour before giving him or her the feed. If he/she wakes up, go to the bedside but do not give him/her anything to eat for half an hour, even though he/she will, of course, scream his/her head off. Reduce the amount of food by 20 ml or breast feed for a minute less. On the next day, go to him/her half an hour later than the time you gave the feed the day before and reduce the amount of food by another 20 ml (or minute of breast feeding) and so on.

If you choose the method which weans the baby from the food first and tackles the problem of his or her repeated waking afterwards, then proceed as follows. Reduce the quantity of food by 20 ml (or one minute of breast feeding) each day and stay at the baby's bedside – without touching him/her – until he/she goes to sleep or stops crying. If you have reached the point when you no longer give any food at night and he/she still wakes up and cries several times, begin to train him/her not to keep waking up: when he/she wakes up and cries, do not go to him/her at once but wait for half an hour. Every two days, postpone the moment when you go to the baby by a further half an hour. The baby will soon learn not to wake up in the night, or rather, he/she will learn to cope using his/her own resources and without outside assistance.

The whole process may sound lengthy and laborious, but it is in precisely such cases that there is great promise of quick success and it is easier to achieve than you imagine. Most children manage to dispense with the night feed (or feeds) within a day or two and sleep right through from the last meal to the next morning without waking.

When babies climb out of bed
What can parents do when older babies, who are quite capable of getting out of bed by themselves, have a problem with going to sleep? This is naturally a lot more difficult and complicated a matter to deal with than the kind of thing that

occurs in infants, but there is no need to worry, for it can be dealt with very successfully.

The principle of the treatment is that parents respond to their children getting out of bed by closing the door of the children's bedrooms for increasingly long periods each time it happens. The children must first and foremost be made to understand that the closed door is the parental response to their getting out of bed without permission. Similarly, they must be able to grasp that the door will be left open if they stay in bed. In the second phase of treatment, they must learn to go to sleep alone and unaided.

How is this achieved in practice?

After children are put to bed, the usual goodnight routine is withheld and instead one of the parents explains that they must go to sleep by themselves. After that, the parent leaves the room without shutting the door.

If the parents hear their children getting out of bed after they have gone into the next room, they must go back into their children's room, put them back into bed and tell them that the door will be closed if they try to get out of bed again. If they do get out of bed again, the parents go to the room once more, put the children back into bed and close the door for one minute. (You can time this on your watch.) The door should not be locked, just held closed in case the children try to get out.

After the door has been closed for one minute, the parents should go into the room again, put the children back to bed, and then leave. The door stays open, but only as long as the children stay in bed. If they get out of bed again, the door is closed for a second time, this time for about two minutes. If the children do not give in, the exercise should be repeated, with the door closed for three minutes, then for four minutes.

This procedure should be continued until the children stop getting out of bed. If they finally comply and stay in bed after the door has been closed for four minutes, it should be open and the children given a few encouraging words from the doorway. Parents can also have a conversation with their children but they take care not to go into their children's room before they have finally dropped off to sleep.

When children wake up during the night, a similar

procedure is recommended. Parents should go to their children's bed, calm them down, but miss out the usual goodnight routine. Then they should leave the room and stand outside the open door. If the children get out of bed again, they should be put back with a caution the first time; after that, the door should be closed whenever they get out of bed, at first for one minute and gradually up to four minutes. But be careful: when children are capable of leaving their beds under their own steam, training methods and reactions are much more difficult than in the case of smaller babies who are confined to their cots. The treatment is wearing and can create a lot of tension, parents being at the mercy of their children's obstinacy. It all requires great patience on the part of mothers and fathers.

When children get out of bed the first time, they must be put back firmly and vigorously without being hurt and without parents showing any anger, however much they may be 'boiling' inside. Whatever the circumstances, they must keep control. Parents then should explain to their children quietly and calmly that they have to learn to sleep by themselves and that the parents cannot stay by their bed all night. They should also be told that the parents will see them again in the morning when they wake, when they will be rewarded with love and attention for being so good.

On the second day, the door should be closed for two minutes in the first instance. This is lengthened by one minute each time to a maximum of four minutes. On the third day, parents can begin with three minutes and increase it each time by a minute to a maximum of five minutes. This is also the limit to keep to in the days following. Parents can talk to their children from outside their rooms to calm them and assure them that the door will be opened again if they go back to bed and settle down. Locking or bolting the door and any other forcible disciplinary methods serve only to frighten children, and are therefore pointless.

Parents will perhaps have to go to their children's bed several times during the first night, calming them down and putting them back. Without doubt, a long and wearing battle is in store. This is an age at which children are perfectly capable of getting out of bed by themselves, yet the punishment options are severely restricted. It is the most problematic age for bringing up children, instilling good habits in them and curbing their thirst for freedom; it is certainly much more difficult than dealing with a helpless baby who simply lies in bed. But don't despair: with consistency and occasional firmness when required, even the most difficult cases can be treated successfully.

If children continue to get out of bed and parents close the door according to the plan, the children will understand better than their parents can imagine that the closing of the door is a result of their unacceptable behaviour. They will eventually comply with the terms as laid down and come to understand that, if they want the door to be left open, it is not worth getting out of bed. But since children are also only human, and there is no universal rule, parents must be prepared for different reactions in each individual case. Some children catch on quickly; others, particularly the obstinate ones, learn to obey more slowly, but eventually even they will have to come to terms with the unalterable facts of life.

There is an alternative to the procedure with the door; a low gate can be fixed to the doorway of the children's room, which will prevent them getting through, climbing over or crawling under. A barred wooden gate is the ideal solution for this: it maintains the children's contact with other family members, is less frightening than a door they can't see through, and it achieves the same purpose – that of preventing the children from leaving the room.

The training aspect is subject to the same rules: parents go into the room, put the children back into bed and proceed according to the schedule detailed above, only this time the wooden gate is closed instead of the door. At the age of three to three-and-a-half, a calendar and stars can also be used as an encouragement: each time the children are able to do without their parents and stay in bed, a star is placed on the calendar; and when a certain number of stars have been achieved, they receive a reward. It is more sensible to give children lots of little rewards than to promise something large and valuable for which they will have to wait heaven knows how long. In the same way, a piggy bank by the children's bed into which parents drop a few pennies each day is much better than the promise of a bicycle to be given when they are older. In this way, the children will cooperate eagerly and will interpret the exercise as a joint effort to ensure good undisturbed nights.

Dealing with serious disorders

We are concerned here with toddlers who are capable of climbing out of bed and who also seem to be suffering from severe anxiety. If parents are convinced that their children are experiencing *actual fear* of being on their own, aside from the usual uneasiness associated wth getting off to sleep, then the learning process should be conducted in two stages aimed at calming the children and fixing a time limit on their crying before parents re-enter the room to quieten them.

To begin with, one parent sits at some distance from the bed and explains that Mummy or Daddy can't lie in bed with them any longer but is sitting nearby to make them feel happy and secure before they go to sleep. Each time the children get out of bed or try to pull their mother or father into the bed, the parent in question leaves the room and shuts the door – each time for a longer period as in the method outlined above.

When the children get back into bed, or the requisite period for the door to be closed is up and the children are put back to bed, the parent once again sits on a chair some way from the bed and leaves the room only if the children get out of bed again.

In this way, the children immediately grasp that a new condition is being imposed and they will have to learn new rules:

- either they stay in bed and one of their parents sits close by;
- or they get out of bed and have to come to terms with a closed door.

This method also has the advantage of teaching children to overcome their bad habit while one parent is sitting close by and helping them to cope with their fear.

In the second stage, the parent goes out of the room leaving the door open. As before, the door is closed only if the children get out of bed.

As already mentioned, this method is lengthy and complicated – more so than the others – and should be used only in particularly difficult cases when genuine fear is involved. On the other hand, though I cannot recommend it as the initial method for all cases, it does work extremely well. There is no harm in using it on a trial basis to begin with, provided parents have enough time and can summon up the necessary patience.

The broken daily routine

Josie is a three-and-a-half-year-old girl. The main complaint which brought her parents to the doctor was that, for about a year, she had been waking up in the night as bright as a button and playing for two hours or longer. This had been happening up to four times a week.

In answer to specific questions from the doctor, the parents explained the following circumstances that had led to Josie's behaviour:

- Her father was an airline pilot and came home at irregular times.
- Josie tended to get tired during the day and had several sleeps at different times each day.
- She always went to bed for the night at a different time. Sometimes this was as early as 6.00 p.m., but if she slept in the afternoons, she went to bed at around 10.00 p.m. whereupon she generally woke during the night.
- She was in the habit of getting up at different times each morning.
- She ate whenever she liked, and this changed from day to day, depending on when she felt like eating and what sort of routine she had had during the day.
- This daily order of events did not bother the parents unduly since they were used to an ever-varying timetable because of the father's job. They never sat down to family meals together, and a structured daily routine was unusual. The only problem that worried the parents was

that Josie woke in the night and did not let them sleep. This made for an even more broken daily routine insofar as there was a routine at all.

- Josie went to sleep without any goodnight ceremony. Sometimes she fell asleep in the living room without saying goodnight. She had no problem in getting off to sleep, and her parents were emphatic that she was not spoiled in any way. She had not developed any particular habits – she didn't even sleep in the same bed all the time. Nor did she make any special demands, or need her parents to be present while she went to sleep.
- Since Josie did not have to account to anyone, and since there were no set rituals, she had very quickly learned to fall asleep anywhere and anytime she felt like it. She ate whenever she felt hungry since there were, of course, no regular mealtimes in this home.
- When she got up in the night, she was neither frightened nor anxious; nor did she sleepwalk. She made no demands on her parents and was as wide awake as if it were morning. She just clambered out of bed and played.
- During the day, she was tired and dropped off to sleep whenever she needed to, depending on how long she had slept the previous night.

These answers made both the case and the diagnosis abundantly clear to the doctor. Of course, other situations are not always as extreme, and doctors cannot always get answers to their questions to make diagnosis so easy. It is worth noting that the parents, educated people though they were, were not in the least bothered by the lack of a daily routine of which their child's routine should have formed part. Nor did it occur to them that Josie's irregular sleeping and eating habits had anything to do with her waking in the night.

Here are a few points I would like to draw to parents' attention if they want to prevent their children waking at night on account of a broken daily routine. The main factor in such cases is the alteration in young children's sleep times. In Josie's case, the constant changing of the time and length of the afternoon nap made it impossible for her to sleep for a fixed period night after night. In this instance, we can even say that she completely lacked any sort of day/night rhythm. Her afternoon nap took the place of her night sleep and was often the longest sleep in any 24 hours. Even in less extreme cases, it is clear that if children sleep in the afternoon until the early hours of the evening, they do not sleep through the whole night.

Josie's afternoon nap was in itself the final and extreme consequence of a broken routine which started with such insignificant things as irregular meal times, unsuitable times for playing and so on. She also did not have any established goodnight routine, and she dozed off each day in a different place and at a different time. This did not seem to upset her in any way, nor did she have nightmares or bad dreams. Put simply, she got enough sleep, but at times that were not the most convenient for her family.

What can be done to change such a situation, to return such children to a day/night rhythm?

In the first place, a brief goodnight ritual must be established and stuck to uncompromisingly. The children should be put to bed each day at the same time, even when they are not tired. If they cry or try to get out of bed, the 'closed door' system should be employed or the step-by-step method to get children to sleep. It is equally important to give these children their evening meals at the same time each day. They should sit at the table with the rest of the family even when they are not hungry, and they should not be given anything to eat after the evening meal.

It is not a good idea to let children of three and older have an afternoon nap of longer than an hour, and even this should not be in the late afternoon. A nap of this length can be achieved in stages: the children should be woken a quarter of an hour earlier each day, until the nap is down to one hour. This makes is possible to put them to bed 15 minutes earlier each evening. Remember that children of this age do not need to sleep for long during the day; often they can do without naps completely if they have a good sleep at night.

Children of this age should not be allowed sleep at all in the course of the morning. If they are tired and fall asleep, they should be woken after quarter of an hour, even if this is against their will. In this way, the broken daily routine is attacked on all fronts, but in gradual stages. Success is assured if parents proceed patiently and consistently.

Difficulties in getting to sleep

One of the commonest reasons why some children have difficulty in getting to sleep is lack of tiredness. This usually results when they sleep too much during the day or in the hours before bedtime.

It is obvious that, if children wake up from their afternoon nap as late as 6.00 in the evening, they will not be ready to go to bed for the night even at 10.00 p.m. I am sure that almost everyone who has read the previous chapter will be convinced that the step-by-step method of training is the best. The aim is to advance the beginning of the afternoon nap from, say, 4.00 p.m. to 1.00 p.m. If your child is having difficulty in getting to sleep at night, ask yourself if his or her afternoon nap goes on till 3.00 or 4.00 p.m. If this is the case, you must bring it – as well as, of course, the time when you wake your child – forward by a quarter of an hour each day.

If babies wake up from their morning nap between midday and 1.00 p.m., parents must likewise advance this time by a quarter of an hour each day until their babies are waking up around 10.00 a.m. That way the afternoon sleep can be brought forward to between 1.00 and 2.00 p.m. Incidentally, children who have passed their first birthday no longer need a nap in the morning, and parents should gradually teach them to do without.

Parents who come up against difficulties with children getting to sleep should also be aware that excessive tiredness can be one of the causes. They should ask themselves if their children are perhaps sleeping too little. Sometimes if they are allowed to rest for a couple of hours in the afternoon, they are then just tired enough – though not too tired – to be able to get to sleep at night more easily.

There is another reason why babies and children seem to have difficulty in getting to sleep: it may be that they are behaving quite normally and it is simply parents' expectations that are inappropriate. Some babies and children

simply do not need all the sleep that childcare books recommend. In such cases, parents should learn to be flexible
and, by allowing their children to go to bed a couple of hours
later, ease the problem. Don't forget to take into account the
child's entire daily routine and *don't judge their behaviour
simply on the basis of when they get up, when they go to
bed and how they act during the night.*

Before dealing with a sleep problem, it is important to
examine the exact cause or causes which have brought about
the difficulties. You must discover and treat the fundamental
and primary problem and not simply concentrate on the
characteristic symptoms. The problem of children who get
up early and go to bed early is similar to the problem of
children going to sleep late and getting up late the next
morning. In both cases, the children are getting enough sleep;
however when they go to sleep late, they find it difficult to
get up in the morning, and vice versa. This can be very
disruptive for the parents. In both cases, the amount of sleep
during the night is sufficient; it just has to be moved an hour
or two forwards or backwards, and the whole daily routine
has to be shifted accordingly. As long as parents judge the
situation correctly, it should not be difficult to overcome.

The problem of older children going to bed late but having
to get up early is the most difficult to deal with. As we
discovered in earlier chapters, human nature is inclined to
allocate itself a 25–26-hour day. An example of this natural
inclination is the fact that we tend to go to bed later at
weekends and during holidays and to get up later the next
morning. However, parents sometimes come up against situations in which their children go to bed late – at 10.00 p.m.,
for example – but have to get up early to get to school on
time. They make up for this lack of sleep at weekends or by
having a nap during the day. Parents are advised to pay
attention to such manifestations when they try to 'postpone'
their children's bedtime.

It is well known that everyone has his or her own particular body rhythm, and it may be that children are unable to
get to sleep early because this does not match their own
daytime rhythm. When they have to, they simply can't, and
this in turn can lead to secondary problems: anxiety, fear of

going to sleep, conflict and a deep uneasiness at the thought of having to lie awake in bed for hours.

So how can parents help their older children alter an established day/night rhythm? All meal times and all sleep times, including those during the day, must gradually be adapted. Each day, sleep time should be shortened by a quarter of an hour either by advancing or delaying the period of sleep. It is very difficult – in fact, practically impossible – to accustom children to going to bed earlier or getting up later than they are used to. Therefore treatment is begun by reducing the duration of sleep by a quarter of an hour. In the initial stages, children are allowed to go to bed as late as they like, and once they have got used to this, they are woken up a quarter of an hour earlier each day, adjusting their normal sleep time during the day accordingly. In this way, parents gain an added advantage: the problems which their children may experience at bedtime, such as conflicts and anxieties, cease to exist even in the very early stages of treatment. If children go to bed when they are tired, the problem solves itself, and by means of this step-by-step approach, bedtime difficulties can be cleared up within two weeks. They must not forget that the entire daily routine has to be adapted at the same time! The treatment progresses in stages of a quarter of an hour each day or every other day.

There is one more relevant point: always remember that humans' natural inclination is to postpone the time for going to bed. Parents should therefore try to prevent their children from succumbing to this natural tendency after successful treatment. Holidays and long weekends, as well as illnesses during which children have to spend lengthy periods in bed, tend to re-establish the former undesirable state of affairs. Be warned!

Early waking

This problem is encountered at all ages. In the case of children, it occurs most frequently between the ages of one to one-and-a-half years – so conspicuously so that we may treat this condition as a normal age-related sleep problem, not as a serious disorder. By acknowledging early waking as quite normal, we are spared having to treat it. This is just as well since it is almost impossible to deal with by the usual training methods.

To me at any rate, it seems impossible to stop energetic, enterprising one-and-a-half-year-olds from waking up at 5.00 a.m., or indeed to persuade them by any means whatsoever to go back to sleep. You will notice that I have refrained from mentioning definite times that could be construed as 'early waking'. This is because I am unable to say with any certainty that at such and such a time in the morning we are dealing with a problem, but after that time everything is all right. I have deliberately avoided stating precise times.

There is a joke about a 40-year-old man who went to his doctor and said: 'I have a problem, doctor. Every morning I have to go to the loo at seven o'clock exactly.'

'So what's the harm in that?' the doctor tried to reassure him. 'That isn't a problem. In fact it's an excellent thing for your bowels to move at the same time each day.'

'Yes, I know,' the patient agreed, 'but in my case I don't wake up till 7.30 a.m.'

The analogy is this: in the case of a farming family, for example, there is no problem if children get up at 5.30 a.m. when the parents are getting up anyway at 5.00. However, in other families where the parents do not get up until 7.00 a.m., there is a definite problem if their children wake at 5.30 a.m.

The business of getting up in the morning is generally a subjective matter for parents; it can hardly be classified as a child's sleep problem. But how are we to deal with babies who wake unusually early and rouse the whole family?

We must, first of all, examine the environmental factors which apply at the time. For example, it is particularly important to check that children's rooms are completely screened from light and noise from outside. The room temperature is equally important; it should be neither too hot nor too cold. All these factors have a direct bearing on, and could interfere with, babies' morning sleep. Sometimes it is enough simply to deal with these factors for the problem to be overcome.

All the same, children's sleep patterns should as a rule be examined and possibly revised. It is a good idea to put them to bed as late as possible, even extending their afternoon nap a little. After they have become accustomed to going to sleep later – say 9.00 or 9.30 p.m. – parents have to wait patiently for a few days to ascertain whether the problem has been remedied. This will not always be the case.

Of course, parents should also check that their children's waking excessively early is not connected with some conditioned habit, such as sucking a bottle or being breast fed in the morning. Babies like this may have acquired good sleeping habits and yet feel 'peckish' in the early morning simply because they have been used to taking nourishment at that time. The treatment consists of postponing giving them their first bottle of the day or their first breast feed by a quarter of an hour every other day. With a great deal of patience, it may be that the problem can be overcome in this way.

But what should parents do if these efforts fail? What if their babies, in spite of all this well-intentioned advice, continue to wake up at 5.00 a.m. bursting with energy and a spirit of adventure?

Some childcare experts claim to be able to help parents solve even this aggravating problem. Their advice is to stagger the treatment by tackling it in stages, exactly as we have dealt with the other sleep problems. The recommended treatment, outlined below, takes three weeks and, judging from past experience, it should ultimately be successful. It works really because it is the only alternative. But the question remains: is it worth all the trouble? Wouldn't it be better to wait and let things take their course until the problem disappears of its own accord?

This is one of the most obstinate problems confronting childcare experts in their search for methods of treatment. But the problem itself does not tend to worsen; on the contrary, it clears up by itself in due course. I would therefore suggest that it should not be treated at all. But if parents are absolutely determined to treat it, then they proceed as follows.

For the first few days, they should go to their children's bedside only after they have been left to cry for a little while. Parents should soothe them gently and affectionately, but quite firmly, and try to explain that it is still night-time and that they have to go on sleeping until morning. They should not lift up their children, not even if their nappies are wet. Instead, they should distract their attention with some toys lying on the bed and leave the room. Parents shouldn't linger outside the room or rush back at the slightest protest, but go back only after 15 minutes. There will, of course, be howling and screaming, but this will abate by and by.

During the second week, parents should not go near their children's bedside at all; instead, they should leave them alone for 15 minutes, regardless of how they react. After that, parents can go in to them and start the normal daily routine. Once again, they will have to have strong nerves to endure the screaming, but in the course of the following days, the noise should decrease. After a further week, they can extend the time a little between the children waking up and their appearing in their room. This should be done progressively until parents have managed to get their children to wake up at a more acceptable hour. I wish them every success!

Sleep problems

Such disorders should be diagnosed and treated only by experts.

The most frequent cause is extreme anxiety. Children may fear for their own lives as the result of a death in the family, some terrible danger, a case of suicide, a long traumatic stay in hospital and so on. Apart from sleep problems, they usually experience other symptoms such as sobbing, a refusal to eat, great shyness, regressive behaviour (e.g. bedwetting after toilet training has been completed), nervousness and a slowing down in activity. There are three types of sleep problems: difficulty experienced in getting to sleep, excessively early rising, and waking in the middle of the night. All three may occur together so that, in some cases, the difficulties in getting to sleep are found in conjunction with waking in the middle of the night.

An ostensible sleep problem may also serve as a convenient device to mask or suppress other psychological problems.

The onset of puberty is notorious for the display of such symptoms. There is an increased tendency to put off going to sleep until late and to get up correspondingly late in the morning; or, as previously mentioned, to put back the timetable of the entire day by an hour or two. During puberty, this quite normal tendency combines with certain predispositions towards emotional problems associated with that age, often depression. This combination may produce a delicate and dangerous condition: some children, usually girls, feel depressed and withdraw from contact with play-mates and schoolfriends, or sometimes cut themselves off entirely from the outside world. They avoid going to school and so on, and in order to justify their conduct to their parents, they develop a sleep problem: they go to bed late and are then unable to get up in time for school. In this way, they succeed in staying at home, explaining their missed schooling in terms of being 'unable to get up' because of sleepless nights. This condition should be recognized in good time and treated without delay by a psychiatrist.

It is by no means unusual that psychological problems should conceal themselves in such ingenious hiding places. It is therefore important to be fully aware of the possibility and be prepared to have such aberrant cases treated accordingly, since the normal treatment for routine sleep problems is fundamentally different.

6
Bedwetting

To remain dry throughout the night is a very difficult, not to say impossible, undertaking for some children. Although bedwetting is classified in medical terms as one of the least serious sleep disturbances, it is one of the most difficult problems to treat and one that can inconvenience the whole family the most.

It belongs to the group of age-related sleep disorders, not to those with pathological causes. All the same, the psychological and sociological consequences of this 'normal' disorder adversely affect children's self-confidence and can lead to further damage. Bedwetting causes children more misery than all the sleep problems mentioned in this book put together. Small wonder then that this is the only problem where children *themselves* long for a solution and actively seek help.

Parents who are familiar with the problem will not be disappointed if I spare them a description of the symptoms and the related stress, and move on instead to certain particulars. How often does this problem occur, and at what point does it merit the designation of 'a genuine problem'? Here are some statistics:

- 50 per cent of two-and-a-half-year-olds still wet the bed at night.
- Among three-year-olds, this applies to 'only' 25 per cent.
- Of four-year-olds, 13 per cent wet the bed every night, 20 per cent wet it several times a week and 25 per cent wet it occasionally.
- With five-year-olds, 15 per cent still wet the bed nightly.
- With six-year-olds, the number falls to 10 per cent.
- With eight-year-olds, it is 8 per cent.

- With 12-year-olds, it is 'only' 3 per cent.
- With 18-year-olds, it is 1 per cent.

In other words, during the second year of primary school, three or four children in every class still wet the bed at night. The age of six is usually taken as the borderline: beyond that, bedwetting is classified as a pathological disorder. To avoid unnecessary semantics, I prefer to leave readers to select their own definition based on the particulars at their disposal. At any rate, they should bear this in mind: *there is no reason why a five- or six-year-old should still be wetting the bed!*

The trouble can be treated and there are good prospects of getting to grips with it. The treatment is simple, effective and, in the majority of cases, successful.

What are the causes of bedwetting?

The medical profession does not offer a reliable answer to this question. In spite of all the research carried out all over the world, no firm conclusion has been reached as to why some children are unable to stay dry at night.

It is far more important and more useful to be certain of what does *not* cause bedwetting. Apart from a very insignificant percentage of bedwetters, the problem does not stem from any disorder in the urinary canal. *It is also important to realize that the problem of bedwetting is not psychologically conditioned.* Bedwetting children are as healthy and well developed and have just as normal personalities as their playmates of the same age. They do not have any health problems.

Having said that, what are the reasons to which bedwetting can be attributed? It is assumed that there are three main factors at work: too small a bladder; insufficient control and sleeping too deeply.

Anatomically speaking, the bladders of bedwetters are not actually small, but these children are not capable of retaining as much urine as others. As far as being less able to control the flow of urine is concerned, the capacity to 'contain oneself' does not seem to be sufficiently developed in these children.

As for sleeping too deeply, a widespread popular view should be dispelled: namely, that bedwetting takes place during the dream phase of sleep. This is simply not true! The exact opposite is the case: in the course of a particularly deep sleep, it sometimes seems to bedwetters that they have dreamed about urinating, but what has in fact happened is that they have only become aware of having wet the bed on waking up. The bedwetting actually happened during an earlier phase of sleep, the so-called deep sleep phase, but bedwetters notice only it during the transition to the subsequent dream phase, when they are woken up by the wetness. In other words, the dream results from the wetness without having been its cause.

Considerable significance should be attached to the heredity factor. It is not actually known how it influences bedwetting, but the statistical data speak for themselves. If both parents were bedwetters up to a relatively advanced age – let's say, over six – there is an 80 per cent probability that their children will also be bedwetters at more or less the same age. If only one parent had this problem, the probability of bedwetting goes down to 40 per cent.

Treating bedwetting

But why should we rack our brains over reasons and conjectures? After all, the main thing is the answer to the question: *How can we get rid of the problem?* .

Methods of treatment are as numerous as theories about what causes the problem. In the former area, however, the outlook is much more encouraging. There are excellent ways and means of treating bedwetting and, in most cases, they are successful, provided they are carried out precisely and consistently. Many parents who have used one of these methods on their own initiative before taking their children to see a specialist have been satisfied with the results. Others have tried all sorts of methods and have met with no success, but a proportion of children are cured of the problem without going further than their GP's waiting room.

Who to go to for treatment

The treatment of bedwetting at night is exclusively a matter for the family doctor or a paediatrician. Under no circumstances should you consult a psychologist or psychiatrist about it, or any other medical or paramedical specialist. Children who wet their beds are not suffering from any psychological problem, and even if the psychologist deals with the bedwetting using the same methods as the family doctor or paediatrician, the very fact that the problem has been shifted to the realm of psychology may cause children much greater harm than the problem itself.

Before treatment

Before any treatment, you should first have your child undergo a routine physical examination, including a general urine test to establish the specific gravity of the urine. Further medical examinations, X-rays and so on are unnecessary.

In the meantime, what should children who wet the bed wear at night? After they have reached the age of four (or even earlier, if the children wish) parents should stop putting them in nappies. These will make them feel that they are still babies, and will also be difficult for them to take off when they have wet them or, indeed, if they want to urinate in the lavatory. Two pairs of thick pants will be enough to absorb all the urine.

How should the bed be protected? If a mattress becomes soaked in urine, the subsequent smell will be unpleasant. Guard against this by putting an oilcloth (or a nylon or rubber sheet) under the sheet, and, in winter, placing a layer of synthetic waterproof material between a duvet and its cover. You can air the bed in the morning to dry it. It is not necessary to wash the sheet every day because urine is sterile, and to get rid of the smell you need only put it in the wash twice a week.

Treatment

There are three methods of treatment which parents can try, and two of them can be used in conjunction.

Method I: boosting self-confidence

The first method is to boost children's self-confidence while letting them take responsibility for curing the problem themselves.

Children – and parents, too – must be convinced that there is no question of any health or psychological defect. Talking to the family doctor can help here, if parents have not concluded this for themselves after reading this book.

It should be made clear to children that they are not to blame for their bedwetting problem. Parents should not be angry with them about it, and, of course, they should not punish them or laugh at them or make them feel ashamed in any way. The attitude of parents *vis à vis* their children must be wholly positive. They should explain to their children that bedwetting is the result of their bladders not being capable of holding enough urine or not yet sufficiently developed. Some parents can even take the whole 'blame' on to themselves and try to explain to their children that bedwetting is something that runs in the family and that they used to wet the bed, too, at the same age. The children must be convinced that their problem can be solved without any particular difficulty, but also that they *must cooperate* at all stages of treatment. All methods of treatment have good prospects for success, provided that the parents know how to strengthen the children's belief that they themselves can get rid of this distressing habit. In the end, success depends wholly on the *children's own will* and on the extent of their collaboration and effort. After all, parents have no control over the functioning of their children's bladders.

Children can be motivated by having a star put on a wall calendar beside their beds every time there has been a dry night. After five stars have gone up, a different coloured star is glued on, which will entitle the children to a small reward. Likewise, some coins can be put in the children's piggy bank for every dry night; after five consecutive dry nights, they are allowed to buy a toy with the money that has accumulated. If the calendar with the reward stars is shown to the doctor, his or her approval can sometimes have a motivating effect. This method of putting responsibility for the treatment's success on to the children themselves, while encouraging them and using other aids geared to positive motivation, is in itself likely to bear good results. It can also be used in conjunction with any other treatment you choose.

Children must also take responsibility for failures. They should not really be punished for 'wet' nights, of course, but they can be given unpleasant duties, such as hanging the wet sheet out on the line, putting it in the washing machine or tumble dryer, changing their wet pyjamas by themselves, washing themselves and so on. They should also be encouraged to wake up at night, even after they have already wet the bed. They should wake up completely and change the sheet themselves that same night.

Method II: improving the working of the bladder
The second method is designed to test the working of children's bladders and their ability to hold back the flow of urine.

As part of developing the bladder function, children should drink a lot. Intake of liquid is the best way of establishing the bladder's functioning capacity. Having a large quantity of urine also helps with other training methods, as they can be practised more often. Drinking a lot should be restricted to the morning; in the afternoon and particularly towards evening, less should be drunk. On average children should drink one glass of liquid per hour in the morning – i.e. six glasses up to 2.00 p.m., and afterwards less, although they should never be forced to remain thirsty. It is self-evident that they should not get into the habit of drinking excessively in the evening, at least not during this treatment, so they should not eat juicy foods such as watermelon at night, or drink anything after their evening meal just for the sake of drinking.

In addition, children should practise their bladder function.

Method III: warning bell

I am aware of all the objections to this method, beginning
with the unfounded argument that the electricity involved
could lead to electrocution of the child, down to the complaint that it can cause personality disorders, burn the penis
and so on. One also occasionally hears the objection that it
does not train children to stay dry but rather to wake up
during the night to urinate.

You should disregard all these views and believe me when
I tell you that this is a very effective method of combating
nightly bedwetting. Thanks to the invention of the warning
bell, the whole problem has acquired a new dimension and
is no longer classified as a disorder detrimental to health.

The mechanical principle of the appliance is simple. The
alarm bell is installed in two separate units. The first is
situated at the spot where the child wets the bed and is
connected by means of an electric cable to a second unit
which contains the bell (or buzzer), the batteries and the
control unit. The instrument is powered by four 1.5 volt
batteries – six volts in all. There is no more danger of electrocution than with an ordinary pocket torch. There are two
types of alarm bell appliances. With one, the child lies on a
sheet, under which there is a large piece of aluminium foil,
covered with an oilcloth pierced with holes. With the other,
the unit which detects the wetness consists of a weak electric
circuit in a small cloth bag attached to the child's pants or
pyjama trousers. The circuit is completed when it becomes
wet and activates the bell.

*The technical principle in all types of these alarms is that
the bell is activated every time it becomes wet.*

The psychological/medical principle behind the method is
to encourage the child to acquire a *conditioned habit*. We
have seen throughout this book that familiar noises, or noises
we are inclined to be aware of because we expect them, can
wake us up. With an alarm bell, as soon as children wet the
bed during the night, the bell rings and they wake up. With
time, they develop a conditioned reflex to the bell: need to
urinate → ringing of bell → waking up. In this way, they
learn to wake up every time they need to urinate during the
night, even before the bell rings. Since waking up is not

exactly pleasant for them, they will be made subconsciously to acquire the ability to contain themselves and to increase the capacities of their bladders. Even at the initial stage, children learn to get up at night to urinate before they wet their beds, and subsequently they also learn to sleep through the whole night without wetting their beds or having to get up at all. Children who stop wetting the bed right at the beginning of treatment do not even reach the intermediate stage of getting up at night.

At what age can this treatment be begun? In the past, it was customary to fix eight years old as the lowest age limit for using this method; before the age of eight, the other methods mentioned above were used. Later, however, the age limit was lowered to six. However, my colleagues and I have successfully treated many children of three-and-a-half to four years old. Chronological age should not, in my opinion, be taken as an indicator of whether or not to use this method, nor is age a factor by which success or failure can be measured. The all-important factor is children's psychological maturity, whether or not they are very childish, and above all, whether they are distressed by bedwetting and how far they are prepared to take an active part in the treatment. Very immature children are not likely to feel that bedwetting is a troublesome disturbance; as a consequence, they are not prepared to collaborate and do not want to make the effort to be dry. Without this readiness, however, we cannot be sure of success, since the child's participation is a prerequisite of all methods of training against bedwetting.

How is the treatment carried out? Children should drink a lot during the morning, an average of one glass (0.25 litre/9 fl. oz) per hour. Conversely they should drink as little as possible towards evening. They should fix the wall calendar beside their bed *by themselves* and put a star on it for every 'dry' night. They should not be too tired when they go to bed (though this is not always so easy to arrange), and before going to sleep, they must install the alarm – again *by themselves* – and demonstrate their own readiness to get up as soon as they hear the bell ring. While they are still dry, they should practise what to do as soon as they hear the bell ringing: stop urinating, wake up completely, get up, turn on the light, switch off the alarm, go to the lavatory and finish urinating there, even if there is not much urine left in the bladder. Then they should hang up their wet pyjama trousers or nightgown to dry on a prepared washing line (or on a radiator) and the sheet, too, if necessary.

For the first few days, parents should be standing by, ready to wake the children at the first sound of the bell. The children must *wake up completely* and consciously register the sound of the bell, as well carrying out all the other actions in the prearranged order, with or without the help of their parents. The appointed goal is for the children to wake up completely, hear the bell and go to the lavatory. Two very common mistakes on the part of the parents often creep in at this stage, and they have been the cause of many failed attempts at treatment:

- Many parents maintain that their children do not hear the bell and so do not wake up. Unfortunately, nobody advised them to wake their children to start off with, and it is this 'little' mistake that makes the great difference between success and failure.
- An even more widespread mistake is that the parents 'rush' their children to the lavatory when the bell rings – sometimes even carrying them in their arms – and without waiting until they are *fully awake*. In this state of semi-sleep – with one eye open and one shut – the children urinate in the direction indicated by their parents. The main thing for these parents seems to be that the bed is not wet; the children simply carry on sleeping. Sometimes they cannot remember anything about it in the morning, so the treatment misses its point completely and all efforts are doomed to failure.

Parents must remember that the purpose of the treatment is to *fully wake children while they urinate*. This is in order to induce a conditioned state, which works as follows: need to urinate → waking up → goal = remaining dry.

In the initial states, children are not yet able to be wakened by the bell. Parents complain that the bell wakens everyone in the house except the one it is supposed to. And they are quite right, because only these children are in the phase of deepest sleep, which is exactly when they urinate, and they are really not able just at that moment to jump up immediately. This is precisely the reason why parents must help them! (Help them to wake up, that is, not to do anything else.) Although within a few days the children will learn to wake themselves, to start with they will need some time to do so, and in the meantime, the bed will get wet. Soon, however, they will learn to get up at the first drop of urine and then the dry nights will begin, and then – what joy! No more drying sheets at night or sleeping on wet ones!

This joy is quite justified and comes not a moment too soon, and even if it is only a case of partial success, it contributes to the children's motivation and makes their families very happy. However, it should be remembered that, for the time being, success is not absolute and there are still some rough patches in store along the way. There may still be many, many wet nights after the first dry ones and even the occasional completely soaked bed. Don't despair, however. This is part of the natural process, and disappointment often follows on the heels of the first encouraging signs of success. *A propos* of this, many specialists recommend that parents set the alarm again after the first bedwetting, so that if it should be repeated, children will wake up again. I am not in favour of this: setting the alarm again after the bed and bedclothes have already become wet is very troublesome, and the bell often goes off even without the bed being wet again. In my experience, there is no doubt that the alarm bell method is successful, even with children who wet the bed more than once a night and who put the alarm on *only once*.

There is another mistake which can cause a lot of worry and negative results after children have become 'dry': breaking off the treatment too soon. After being followed for two successive weeks, when children are wetting the bed only once or twice a week, the treatment reaches a new phase: now the children must be given a lot to drink in the afternoon and towards evening too, while the alarm treatment is continued. A succession of bedwetting occurrences may follow because of the excessive drinking, but this will ensure fewer lapses in future. Continue this further stage until four weeks have elapsed without any bedwetting. After three or four weeks of dry nights (during which the children drink a lot), the therapy can be reckoned to have succeeded. If, after a period of time, the children begin to wet the bed once more, it is advisable to put the alarm bell back into use for a short time. With perseverance, the problem will finally solve itself.

The alarm bell method of treatment has revolutionized the treatment of this unpleasant nocturnal phenomenon. Although bedwetting is a troublesome and serious problem and should not be taken too lightly, it can, however, be overcome. With conscientious and consistent training, it is possible to eliminate bedwetting in 70–85 per cent of sufferers within an average of three months!

Treatment with medicines

Treatment with medicines can only be authorized by a doctor. Thanks to the alarm bell treatment, drug treatment has now been superseded, although it should not be dismissed altogether, as it undeniably produces a certain degree of success, too. The most effective drug is Tofranil (imipramine) in tablet form. Treatment is begun with a very small dose – one tablet one hour before sleep. Children take one tablet every day until they have managed one completely 'dry' month. After this, it is advisable to stop taking the drug only gradually: in the first week of the second month, the tablet should only be taken once every two days, and then at longer intervals until it is completely stopped. On the other hand, if one tablet does not prove effective, the dose can be doubled (with the doctor's agreement), but in this case, treatment should not continue for longer than two months. This type of treatment is suitable only for children already over the age of six. Doctors still do not quite understand how the tablets work (they are prescribed for adults as antidepressants), but the treatment is a great help to many children. It is only a pity that the percentage of successes is not higher and that the number of relapses after a completed course of tablets is quite considerable.

It is important to emphasize that with this particular treatment children are naturally inclined to remain almost passive.

They think the tablets are taking over the 'work' for them. For this reason, parents should be even more careful to see that their children keep exactly to the treatment rules – for example, fixing the appropriate stars on the wall calendar, drying their night clothes themselves and so on.

Treatment with drugs occasionally results in side-effects, such as difficulties with sleeping and even nightmares, nervousness and changes in behaviour. With the proper dosage, however, these phenomena seldom occur. Parents should also beware of the most serious side-effect of all: an overdose of tablets. The tablets' colour (red-brown) and shape (either triangular or round) are tempting to children, and when this method of treatment was very widely used for a time in Britain these tablets were the most frequent cause of drug overdose in children.

For this very reason, it is advisable to take precautions, so that other little children in the family do not get access to what they may think are 'sweeties'. Parents must keep the tablets out of reach of children undergoing treatment, too. There have been cases in the past where children, frustrated at still wetting their beds, have taken a double or triple dose in the belief that this will speed up the cure. Let this be a warning to all parents!

Index